DID YOU KNOW
YOU CAN TAKE ON THE CHALLENGE WITH YOUR WHOLE CHURCH?

ALL-IN, TURNKEY SERMON SERIES WITH PROVEN RESULTS!

WWW.FORGIVINGCHALLENGE.COM/CHURCH

WANT YOUR PASTOR TO RECEIVE A FREE COPY?

EMAIL HELLO@REDLETTERCHALLENGE.COM

ACKNOWLEDGMENTS

Forgiving Challenge was a team effort. I'm so grateful to so many who have contributed in some way.

Thank you, Jesus! We simply would not have a book like this had You not went to the cross and paid the price for us. Thank you, Father, for sending your one and only Son. Thank you, Holy Spirit, for giving me the words to share and allowing me to be a fellow worker in bringing God's kingdom to earth right now.

Allison, you know me more than anyone else. You've seen me at my weakest. And yet, you show me grace. You forgive me. You give me second chances. You are the embodiment of Jesus in my life, and I'm forever grateful to you.

Nathan and Brady, you continue to provide me with great content! More than that, it's a joy to watch you both grow in the grace of Jesus. Thank you for the privilege of being your "dad."

Thank you to the *Red Letter Living* team, especially Andrea Miller and James Saleska. Your thoughts and gifts have contributed immensely.

Thank you to the Quadrivium Group, Steve and Susan Blount, for your continued belief in our projects. Thank you, Doug Peterson, for your masterful touches. Thank you, PlainJoe Studios, for making this project come to life like nobody else can!

Thank you to those in my family, as well as friends and fellow pastors, who reviewed this book for me—Mark and Sharon Zehnder, Ryan Carlson, Jacob Baumann, Aaron Hutton, Mark Crossman, Tom Pfotenhauer, Greg Griffith, and Mark Schulz. Your insights truly helped. I love you all so much.

TABLE OF

CONT

ACKNOWLEDGMENTS • • • • • • • • • • 3

INTRO • • • • • • • • • • • • • • • • 6
SCARS AND SECOND CHANCES

S.C.A.R.S.
DAY 1: SIN • • • • • • • • • • • 22
DAY 2: CONFESSION • • • • • • • 26
DAY 3: ABSOLUTION • • • • • • • 30
DAY 4: RESTORATION • • • • • • 36
DAY 5: SANCTIFICATION • • • • • 40

SIN
DAY 6 • • • • • • • • • • • • • 46
DAY 7 • • • • • • • • • • • • • 52
DAY 8 • • • • • • • • • • • • • 58
DAY 9 • • • • • • • • • • • • • 62
DAY 10 • • • • • • • • • • • • 68
DAY 11 • • • • • • • • • • • • 74
DAY 12 • • • • • • • • • • • • 80

CONFESSION
DAY 13 • • • • • • • • • • • • 88
DAY 14 • • • • • • • • • • • • 96
DAY 15 • • • • • • • • • • • • 104
DAY 16 • • • • • • • • • • • • 108
DAY 17 • • • • • • • • • • • • 114
DAY 18 • • • • • • • • • • • • 120
DAY 19 • • • • • • • • • • • • 126

ENTS

ABSOLUTION

DAY 20	134
DAY 21	140
DAY 22	146
DAY 23	152
DAY 24	158
DAY 25	164
DAY 26	170

RESTORATION

DAY 27	178
DAY 28	182
DAY 29	188
DAY 30	194
DAY 31	200
DAY 32	206
DAY 33	212

SANCTIFICATION

DAY 34	220
DAY 35	226
DAY 36	232
DAY 37	238
DAY 38	244
DAY 39	250
DAY 40	256

THE FINAL CHALLENGE · · · 262

ABOUT THE AUTHOR	266
BIBLIOGRAPHY	267
#CHAPTER89	270

INTRODUCTION:

SCARS & SECOND CHANCES

It happened so fast that I didn't have time to take evasive action. I barely had time to think. There wasn't even time for my life to flash in front of my eyes.

All I can remember was seeing, out of the corner of my eye, a black pickup truck coming straight for my driver's door at tremendous speed. Then the crunch of twisting metal, the crackle of breaking glass, the WHOOMPF of the billowing airbag, and darkness.

Almost instantly, I lost consciousness.

The day was July 31, 2001—the transition summer between high school and my first year at Concordia University near Milwaukee. The Zehnder family was having a reunion in Angola, Indiana, and I was behind the wheel as we drove back from hitting some golf balls at a driving range. My older brother and a cousin were in the back seat, while another cousin was in the front passenger seat.

As I entered this intersection, I was completely unaware that I had just run through a stop sign. The car in front of me didn't stop, so I assumed there was no stop sign—a dumb mistake. The cross traffic did not have to stop, so when I entered the intersection, I was blindsided by a pickup going close to 60 miles per hour.

I remember coming back to consciousness, but only briefly, as my brother said, "Are you all right, Zach?"

I felt all right, although I couldn't move. The pickup truck had struck my door, which caved in, pinching my waist against the center console, where you find the cupholders. I could wiggle only enough to tell that I wasn't paralyzed. But I couldn't free my legs. Then I dropped back into oblivion.

When I regained consciousness, the medics were there, but they couldn't get me out. Back to darkness…

When I came to again, I could hear the mechanical whirr of a tool being used to pry open my door. Emergency workers had arrived on the scene with a "Jaws of Life"—a powerful hydraulic tool with a "spreader" that opens up crunched-in car doors. It's like a can opener on steroids.

I remember mumbling something about whether my brother and cousins were all right, and then it was off to la-la land again.

When I finally returned to consciousness, I remained alert as they transferred me to a stretcher. Shockingly, I felt completely normal and almost wondered if I could have walked to the ambulance. But they weren't taking any chances in such a bad accident.

Authorities had alerted my parents at the reunion and assured them it was no big deal. They really undersold the potential seriousness of the accident. Therefore, my parents were stunned when they arrived on the scene just in time to see me being rolled on the stretcher to the ambulance.

I learned that my brother and cousin in the back seat were all right—although the cousin in the front seat had some bleeding in one ear. It's possible that my head might have struck his ear when the airbag went off. Unfortunately, he lost some of his hearing in that ear. The driver of the pickup truck was fine, and we learned he was from a Christian family. We were enveloped in prayer.

It was a miracle that we all lived and were mostly injury-free. I came out unscathed, except for a little scar on my chin that did not even require stitches.

July 31 became my Second-Chance Day.

I had felt a calling to be a pastor when I was a freshman in high school, but as the years went by, that calling began to fade. I never became part of a wild party scene, but I was beginning to move away from my calling.

The accident was a wake-up call—my Jonah moment.

The prophet Jonah famously ran from his calling, which was to preach repentance to the Ninevites. But God stopped him in his tracks, and Jonah wound up in the belly of a huge fish, where he finally came to his senses. I too wound up trapped in the belly of a beast, except my "beast" was my dad's Honda Accord. Jonah was swallowed by the jaws of the great fish, while I was freed by the Jaws of Life.

But my greatest sense of freedom came that very night, when I got down on my knees and thanked God for His protection. That night, I decided to answer the call to become a pastor, and one week later I enrolled in Concordia's pastoral ministry program.

Today, I am a fourth-generation pastor in the Zehnder family.

DO YOU HAVE A HARDER TIME RECEIVING FORGIVENESS FOR YOURSELF OR GIVING FORGIVENESS TO OTHERS?

When I left the hospital that day in 2001, I was in possession of two things:

1 A TICKET FOR RUNNING A STOP SIGN

2 A SCAR ON THE BOTTOM OF MY CHIN

This scar is precious to me today. It represents the moment when God gave me a second chance at life. Our God is a God of Second Chances…and Third Chances… and Fourth Chances…and…You get the idea.

Our God is a forgiving God. But do we *really* believe it?

One question I often ask people is: Do you have a harder time receiving forgiveness for yourself or giving forgiveness to others? When asking this, I have found the vast majority of people struggle with receiving forgiveness. While we have a long way to go to be more gracious with and forgiving of others, we are typically the least forgiving of ourselves.

This fact leads me to the following conclusion: You cannot be forgiving of others until you have received forgiveness for yourself. We forgive others by learning to receive God's forgiveness for ourselves.

Thankfully, in each of our life stories, someone has taken the initiative to grant us total freedom. His name is Jesus. It may sound surprising, but the primary goal of this book is not to learn how to forgive others. You will be going even deeper to a point that is likely much more difficult and painful. This is primarily a book about receiving God's forgiveness for yourself. I'm all for reconciliation in our society and extending forgiveness to others. But it starts with encountering Jesus. Once you have received the grace of Jesus, it compels you to be forgiving of others.

The scar on the bottom of my chin is a constant reminder to me of God's grace. God's forgiveness. My scar has turned into a powerful, pivotal moment and story—because that's what scars do.

Scars tell powerful stories.

Did you know that the resurrected body of Jesus still carried scars? Scars are a surprising feature of a resurrected body. On the surface, scars seem to be a defect. Wouldn't we expect an upgrade in our resurrected body—one without blemishes, one without any marks of suffering?

So why would God allow the scars of Jesus to remain? Is it so that we would forever remember our sin? To constantly remind us of our guilt and shame? That would be out of character for God. Remember, Romans 8:1 says, **"Therefore, there is now no condemnation for those who are in Christ Jesus."** God doesn't want us to continually dwell on our shortcomings. So what does God want to tell us through the scars of Jesus?

YOU CANNOT BE FORGIVING OF OTHERS UNTIL YOU HAVE RECEIVED FORGIVENESS FOR YOURSELF.

God made scars. They were His idea. He created human skin with the ability to heal, but many times the healing leaves a scar. Some scars may have little meaning to you, but other scars may have a lot to say. The scars of Jesus have the most to say.

The Gospel writers Luke and John both describe the resurrected Jesus bursting into a room filled with His disciples who were quarantined out of fear. Jesus allowed His disciples to see and touch His nail-scarred hands—the evidence they needed to prove it really was Him.

Thomas earned his nickname, "Doubting Thomas," that night. He said, **"Unless I see the nail marks in his hands and put my finger where the nails were, and put my hand into his side, I will not believe." John 20:25**

Jesus responded, **"Put your finger here; see my hands. Reach out your hand and put it into my side. Stop doubting and believe." Thomas said to him, "My Lord and my God!" John 20:27-28**

For as much grief as we give Thomas about his one statement of doubt, he would go on to be an incredible influence for the cause of Jesus. Thomas, by most historical accounts, was the first disciple to bring the Gospel of Jesus to the nation of India and would eventually be martyred for his faith in Jesus.

The scars of Jesus turned a Doubting Thomas into a devoted disciple of Jesus. Likewise, His scars have the ability to mark us and truly change us forever.

The scars of Jesus tell the story of an innocent man, who died a brutal death for guilty sinners. This innocent man was also fully God. Through His death and resurrection, those same guilty sinners receive a free gift of grace that allows them to be in right relationship with God for eternity, now and forever. Not only does this grace usher us into heaven after we die, but it also brings us into a right relationship with Him today. And being in relationship with God in this world allows us to experience great purpose, meaning, and fulfillment.

Pastor and poet Edward Shillito witnessed the horrors of World War I firsthand. As he saw the wounds of his friends and allies, he reflected upon a Jesus who knows about human pain. It led him to write this beautiful poem:

"THE HEAVENS FRIGHTEN US;
THEY ARE TOO CALM;

IN ALL THE UNIVERSE
WE HAVE NO PLACE.

OUR WOUNDS ARE HURTING US;
WHERE IS THE BALM?

LORD JESUS, BY THY SCARS,
WE CLAIM THY GRACE."[1]

– EDWARD SHILLITO

#FORGIVINGCHALLENGE

It's one thing to look at Jesus's scars. It's another to receive from His scars what He truly wants to give you—His grace. His grace forever marks you as God's child. And if that is true, then His grace ought to extend from us to others in this world. You would think that followers of Jesus would be known as the most forgiving and gracious of people. And yet, this is far from reality.

Jesus is known for grace. Christians are known for judgment.

Grace and judgment, by definition, are polar opposites of one another. Grace is getting a free gift you don't deserve. Judgment is getting exactly what you deserve.

I have often struggled with this reality and find it hard to believe that a people associated with Jesus could be so far away from the life and example of Jesus. Something has to change.

We can't just grit our teeth to become more forgiving of others. So, what do we need to do?

> MANY OF US CARRY WOUNDS ON THE INSIDE THAT WE HAVE NOT PROPERLY DEALT WITH.

First, we must understand that on a level much deeper than our physical scars, many of us carry wounds on the inside that we have not properly dealt with or allowed God to heal. We may be the only ones aware of just how many deep wounds we carry. It's possible that these are a result of another person's actions against us, but some of the deepest, darkest hurts are those we may have brought on ourselves.

"Reconciliation" is a word used widely by many secular and spiritual leaders. Reconciliation requires two parties to come together. Each party must walk over to the other side, but I believe it is the Christian's responsibility to take the first step in that direction.

The only problem is that far too many Christians walk to the other side still carrying personal wounds without having dealt with them appropriately. Is it possible that if we are already coming to the table wounded, we could be doing more damage to one another? How can we help solve world problems and injustices if we ourselves haven't experienced true healing and freedom?

To receive total freedom, the first step is knowing that God Himself has truly forgiven you.

Isaiah 53:5 declares: **"But he was pierced for our transgressions, he was crushed for our iniquities; the punishment that brought us peace was on him, and by his wounds we are healed."**

Over the next 40 days, you will experience the incredible forgiveness Jesus offers you. My prayer is that along the journey you will allow God's grace, experienced through His wounds, to heal you. Your wounds will turn into beautiful scars that tell an incredible story about an extraordinary God!

Bring all of your shame; bring all of your guilt. Bring the stuff you've been suppressing—the stuff buried underneath the couch cushions. It's time to pull it all out. And the baggage you've been toting around wherever you go? Bring that, too. Bring it all to Jesus, and if you do, I can promise that you will experience freedom like you never thought possible.

In his book *The Weight of Glory*, I love the way that C.S. Lewis describes the freedom that Jesus offers to us. He says, "We are half-hearted creatures, fooling about with drink and sex and ambition when infinite joy is offered us, like an ignorant child who wants to go on making mud pies in a slum because he cannot imagine what is meant by the offer of a holiday at the sea. We are far too easily pleased."[2] Jesus declares to us in John 10:10b: **"I have come that they may have life, and have it to the full."** There is a battle raging on for your heart and soul, but Jesus assures the victory in that battle.

In fact, it's already been won.

One last thing about that fateful day on July 31. This wasn't just the day that I was almost killed in a car accident. This wasn't just the day God gave me a second chance. And it wasn't just the day when I decided to become a pastor.
July 31 was the day I married Allison—in 2004, three years to the day after the accident. This wasn't planned. In fact, I had no idea that we were getting married on the same life-changing date until my brother brought it up during his best-man speech at our wedding reception. So this truly is a day of redemption for me.

When Jesus returns to redeem all of creation, the Bible sometimes presents it as a wedding, with Jesus as the groom and the Church as His bride. This will be the day when all things are made new—when pains are gone, tears are wiped away, car accidents are a thing of the past, and forgiveness is fulfilled.

When Jesus comes back, maybe He'll even do it on a July 31 sometime in the future. But any day is fine with me.

WHAT WILL THIS 40-DAY CHALLENGE JOURNEY LOOK LIKE?

The answer to every spiritual problem in existence is always to look to Jesus.

And that's exactly what we are going to do in *Forgiving Challenge*. If you struggle to understand God, simply look to Jesus because He reveals the character of God. The best way to learn what true, real, and perfect forgiveness looks like is by examining this question: "How did Jesus forgive?"

There are many powerful stories of Jesus's forgiveness of others in the Bible—a Samaritan woman who met Jesus at the well, a woman caught in adultery, Zacchaeus the tax collector, and a rebellious child known as the Prodigal Son, to name a few. But my favorite story of forgiveness is when Jesus forgives one of His disciples—Peter. Peter is Jesus's right-hand man, which makes the gift of forgiveness all the more meaningful. This book will largely focus on the forgiveness that Jesus gave to Peter.

Over the first five days, I'll introduce you to the Five Phases of Freedom using the acronym SCARS.

SIN

CONFESSION

ABSOLUTION

RESTORATION

SANCTIFICATION

On Days 6 to 40, we will dive deeper into each of the Freedom Phases. Each week, we will look at the unfolding story of Jesus and Peter to better understand our own stories.

DAYS 6-12

The topic of **SIN** and how we miss the mark

DAYS 13-19

The practice and importance of **CONFESSION**

DAYS 20-26

God's declaration of **ABSOLUTION** for every person

DAYS 27-33

God's words of full **RESTORATION** available to all

DAYS 34-40

How to walk in complete freedom through the process of **SANCTIFICATION**

My hope is that after seeing God's forgiveness and freedom offered to Peter, the over-arching challenge in this workbook will be to help you receive God's forgiveness, allowing you to be free.

The greatest impression on humanity remains the scars of Jesus. His forgiveness leaves a greater impact on the world than any of your sins could ever leave. If God's forgiveness has left such a significant signature on humanity, then I wonder if our greatest mark on humanity could be God working and bringing freedom through our own scars.

This will not be an easy process. It will be painful. It will be difficult. But if you persevere and complete the process and receive God's forgiveness, Jesus will bestow more freedom on you than you ever thought possible.

Remember Jesus's words when He opened the scroll in Luke 4:18: **"The Spirit of the Lord is on me, because he has anointed me to proclaim good news to the poor. He has sent me to proclaim freedom for the prisoners and recovery of sight for the blind, to set the oppressed free."**

The one whom Jesus will set free in this 40-day challenge is you.

Dr. Karl Menninger, a well-known psychiatrist and self-proclaimed atheist, once said that if he "could convince the patients in psychiatric hospitals that their sins were forgiven, 75% of them could walk out the next day!"[3]

If an atheist can understand the power of forgiveness, how much more should followers of Jesus!

Welcome to *Forgiving Challenge: A Life-Changing 40-Day Journey to Freedom.* Are you ready?

BEFORE YOU BEGIN

Before you begin your journey, here are a few helpful tips to maximize the impact that this 40-day challenge can have in your life.

1 INVITE SOMEONE TO WALK WITH YOU.

Most of the greatest challenges that are conquered in life are not meant for individuals to tackle alone. Our hope is that you will do this challenge with at least one other person. If you are joining in this challenge with your small group or your church, it's still important that you have one person who can help to hold you accountable for the duration of this challenge. This person should be someone you can trust deeply, is walking as a disciple of Jesus, and is mature in the faith. After finding an accountability partner, identify specifics, such as how often you will check in with one another and what questions you will ask each other at those check-ins.

2 WRITE IT DOWN.

After the first five introductory days, Days 6 to 40 will offer a daily challenge to complete. Because of the inner focus of *Forgiving Challenge*, most of the daily challenges will revolve around specific personal questions to answer. Our hope is that you won't gloss over these and jump to the next day, but that you will spend time being honest with the questions. Francis Bacon once said, "Reading maketh a full man…and writing an exact man."[4] In other words, writing will force you to be more precise in your thoughts. Spending an average of an extra 10 to 15 minutes a day writing your thoughts down will put you in a great place to experience the freedom God has for you!

3 DON'T GIVE UP.

You will not do this challenge perfectly. Give yourself grace. This challenge goes beyond checking boxes just to get it done. It's a challenge that will bring you more fully into the grace, forgiveness, and freedom that Jesus offers. We have found that the most vulnerable day—the day you're tempted to give up—is "the day after perfect." If you miss a day or struggle with a day, don't give up. Instead, give yourself grace and pick up the next day. Keep walking.

4 **SHARE THE WINS.**

Join the thousands of others who are embarking on the journey. Use #ForgivingChallenge at any time on social media to share quotes, stories, or testimonies of what God is doing in your story. Sharing your wins publicly will not only encourage others to do the same, but it will also give people the opportunity to glorify God through your Freedom Journey!

THE 40-DAY FORGIVING CHALLENGE IS ON!

DAY 1

SIN

Sin is a small word that packs a mighty punch.

In a culture where we have become addicted to being offended, one of the most offensive things you could say to someone is that they are a "sinner." We live in a world that likes to accept and affirm all decisions and choices, when in reality, every single one of us is a sinner.

Paul, a follower of Jesus in the first century, declares in Romans 3:10, **"There is no one righteous, not even one."** Later, in verse 23, he elaborates to tell us that **"all have sinned and fall short of the glory of God."**

Without first understanding and accepting that you are a sinner, you will never be free.

But what exactly is sin?

Sin is derived from an old archery term meaning "to miss the mark." If the bullseye is the mark you intend to hit, then technically, anything other than bullseye is considered a sin. If you picture a dartboard, that means that no matter if you throw a dart and hit the Triple 20 or completely miss the board, you have sinned. Any attempt that doesn't hit the intended mark, the bullseye, is a sin.

You can imagine that this is a pretty difficult standard to hit every time. That's exactly my point. You cannot attain the perfect standards that God has set out for you. Even if you just miss a little bit, you still miss.

If you are truly honest with yourself, you have fallen short of what you want for yourself. If you are like me, you have been trying to become a better version of yourself for decades now. You thought that you wouldn't still be dealing with particular sins, bad habits, or addictions. Personally, I am hard-pressed to find anyone in this life who has lied to me or disappointed me more than myself. I know I'm not the only one who feels this way.

And yet, there's a twisted perception of reality that thinks if you just become better and wealthier, buy a better house, get a greater job, just keep improving, etc., then you will be happy and all will be well. I want to remind you that not even the very best version of yourself will ever be good enough for God and will never even fully satisfy you.

The version of yourself in your head, the one with the six-pack abs, cash falling out of your pockets, and a job in a high-rise office, will be just as disappointing to you as the real version of you right now. The version of yourself with the big house, white picket fence, new Tesla, and kids who lead the National Honor Society, will not complete you. You'll find something new about yourself that you don't like. Why? Because you are sinful.

Let me start the freedom experience, as the author of this book, by saying this to you:

"Hi, my name is Zach Zehnder, and I am a sinner."

I have missed the mark. I still miss the mark. And I fully believe, even with right intentions and after receiving the grace of God in my life, I will continue to miss the mark. Sometimes I miss the mark by a little bit. Just barely. Sometimes I miss the mark by a lot. My sins include pride, lust, greed, and wrongful comparison. At times I have been apathetic in my faith, harsh, or even unmerciful to others. I have pursued the god of comfort far too often. I have passed up opportunities to serve others to instead serve myself.

The last thing that I would want you to tell me, if you truly care about who I am, is that you affirm me for who I am fully today. Please don't. Because I am not okay with the wrong parts of me. And as a follower of Jesus, I desperately desire to be a more faithful follower of Jesus. I hate that sin still gets in my way.

The last thing you will hear from me in *Forgiving Challenge* is that I think you are perfect the way you are. You are not. You are sinful. And I would hope that the reason you are reading this book is not so we can have a fake, plastic, inauthentic experience, but so that we can deal with the broken, the messy, and even the worst parts of your story. This is the only way you can truly experience God's freedom, which you may have never thought possible.

Don't hear me wrong. God loves you. Deeply. But He cares about who you are becoming too. Deeply.

God loves you for who you are, but His freedom doesn't leave you just as you are.

In fact, even though the consequence of sin is separation from God, we don't have to remain separated from Him. When we were broken, sinful, and messy, God sent His Son, Jesus, to come and rescue us. God took the first step. Jesus is unafraid of our sin, and He is willing to step into our mess to lift us out.

Psalm 40:2 declares, **"He lifted me out of the slimy pit, out of the mud and mire; he set my feet on a rock and gave me a firm place to stand."**

We have a God who brings freedom to our lives through His ultimate rescue. We have a God who is greater and bigger than sin. I love the lyrics from Elevation Worship's song *Raised to Life:* "Sin was strong, but Jesus is stronger. Our shame was great, but Jesus you're greater."[5]

Just as there is a God who loves you, there is an enemy, the devil, who hates you. He is constantly fighting against you. The devil wants you to stay stuck in your sin, to reflect on it, to be defined by it, to suppress it, and to deny it. Our God is not only greater than sin; He is greater than the devil, too.

Sin can ruin you, but it doesn't have to. The acknowledgement of sin begins the process of freedom that God so desperately wants you to receive.

The admission price into freedom begins with an admission of your sin.

Through the sacrifice of Jesus, not only can your sin be defeated, but what you will see in this challenge is that God can even take the worst parts of our stories, even our sins, and use them for His glory.

This 40-day challenge is for sinners to experience freedom. Welcome, sinner.

On Days 6 to 12, you will be introduced to Peter and the sin for which he is most known. Along the way, you'll be challenged to identify the places and times in which you have missed the mark. Heads up, this will likely be the most painful week. I promise you, though, your pain will have purpose.

DAY 2

CONFESSION

As a result of our sin, all of us are born into this world separated from God. This is known as original sin. But we are also all born with a conscience, which helps us determine right and wrong.

Contrary to popular belief, it is entirely appropriate for us to feel sorrow and guilt after committing a sin. It's appropriate because, in fact, we are guilty. This is the natural response that we ought to experience. The apostle Paul lays out the two options in 2 Corinthians 7:10: **"Godly sorrow brings repentance that leads to salvation and leaves no regret, but worldly sorrow brings death."**

Wow! Paul declares that sorrow can bring either repentance or death. It's what happens after you sin, what you do with your sorrow, that makes all the difference; it determines whether you'll experience freedom or not.

Although people say we live in a "post-Christian" nation, as recently as 2019, the Pew Research Center said that 65 percent of Americans still self-identify as Christians.[6] Collectively, we do not have a problem identifying ourselves with Jesus, but we have a problem truly understanding what a life marked by the grace of Jesus looks like. Sadly, in a nation filled with supposed Christians, few depend on Jesus to overcome sin. LifeWay research found that "only 22% of American men and 33% of American women said they depend on Jesus Christ to overcome sin."[7]

Any pursuit of freedom outside of Jesus will always lead to more bondage.

The devil wants to take your natural feeling of guilt and turn it into lifelong shame. After all, there is a big difference between guilt and shame.

GUILT IS: "I DID SOMETHING WRONG."
SHAME IS: "I AM SOMETHING WRONG."

Guilt brings conviction. God can use guilt to bring us to our knees in confession— and confession is the key that unlocks our prison cell. It brings freedom. Andy Stanley says in his book, *Enemies of the Heart,* that confession has "the potential to free you from your guilt…Remember, the purpose of confession is not to relieve your conscience; it's to effect change and reconciliation."[8]

Shame, on the other hand, brings condemnation. Satan uses shame to imprison us, to condemn us to death. Shame hits at your core identity and leaves you with constant feelings of inadequacy. The devil wants you to carry that shame with you wherever you go.

1 Peter 5:8 (NLT) declares: **"Stay alert! Watch out for your great enemy, the devil. He prowls around like a roaring lion, looking for someone to devour."**

The devil devours you from the inside. He will prowl around and roar at you with false accusations to convince you that you not only did something wrong, but you are something wrong. He will try to place labels on you, and sometimes, sadly, he will even do it through the people who love you. But I know from personal experience that the most negative person speaking to me in this world is not anyone else. It's me. If the devil can get you to carry around that shame, he knows you will never experience the full, abundant life and freedom that Jesus offers to you. Are you going to let the devil win and turn your guilt into shame? If so, how's that been working out for you?

There is another option. You can bring your sorrow, your guilt, and whatever level of shame you are experiencing to Jesus. In Jesus, you will experience His total forgiveness. Instead of elevating your guilt into shame, Jesus will remove your guilt by His grace. And it all starts with a wonderful practice called confession.

Look at what the apostle John says to us in 1 John 1:8-10: **"If we claim to be without sin, we deceive ourselves and the truth is not in us. If we confess our sins, he is faithful and just and will forgive us our sins and purify us from all unrighteousness. If we claim we have not sinned, we make him out to be a liar and his word is not in us."**

John reminds us that every one of us has committed a sin. If you say you haven't, well, John just called you a liar. So there you go. You just lied. Now you can join the rest of us sinners in this challenge!

In the church tradition that I've grown up in, we begin every worship gathering by confessing our sins before God. One time, a gentleman who had come for a few months scheduled a meeting with me. He said he enjoyed many aspects of our church, but he so disliked the practice of confession that he decided he was leaving our church. He explained that it's pointless to make this communal confession because God doesn't want us to remember our sins any longer. He has already paid for them, so to confess like this is not trusting that God has done this mighty work.

I tried to explain to him that the reason we confess our sins before God is not so that we experience more guilt, and certainly not shame. But rather, we do this because confession puts us in a place to ultimately experience God's kindness. Any acknowledgment of our sin—and the sorrow we experience because of it—is an important part of confession, but it is never the end goal. I remember telling this man, "If you walk away from confessing your sins more focused on your own brokenness than on God's kindness, than you have completely missed the point."

Romans 2:4 declares this truth for us: **"Do you show contempt for the riches of his kindness, forbearance and patience, not realizing that God's kindness is intended to lead you to repentance?"**

Repentance is the process of changing, or turning, from a particular sin. Until we truly turn from our sin, we will not experience the full freedom that God wants for us! But remember, it is not through our power, grit, hard work, and perfection, but rather, it is through God's kindness that we will ultimately experience His freedom.

What truly changes us from the inside out is that God has been kind toward us, in spite of our sin. Through His forgiveness, He offers a free gift that you absolutely do not deserve—grace.

In *Recovering Redemption*, Matt Chandler writes, "For what's broken in us—what's aching for recovery—is beyond our ability to fix. And from the moment it broke, all attempts to redeem it by ourselves are doomed to futility and failure. We need God. Or else. Not just once. Not just to get His signature on our heavenly hall pass. But forever. We will never get over needing Him."[9]

When we confess our sins to God, we give Him an opportunity to do His saving work in our lives. We confess our sin to God so that we hear His words of forgiveness over our lives. Without God's forgiveness, it is impossible to experience freedom.

On Days 13 to 19, you will learn about the powerful practice of confession. In confession, you are given the opportunity to experience the kindness of Jesus. You will see that the same kindness Jesus so willingly gave to his friend Peter is also offered to you.

DAY 3

ABSOLUTION

What does it truly mean to be forgiven?

There are two common definitions of the word forgive:

1 TO CANCEL A DEBT

2 TO STOP FEELING ANGRY OR RESENTFUL TOWARD SOMEONE FOR AN OFFENSE, FLAW, OR MISTAKE

When we receive the total forgiveness of God, our debt is canceled and the Lord's righteous anger is gone. God's forgiveness is not either/or. It is both/and.

Today, let's look at the first definition—canceling a debt.

Human beings love justice and law stories. Just look at how many *CSI, NCIS,* and *Law and Order* shows there have been. It doesn't take too much creativity to add one of these shows to network television. Slap a new city on it (LA, New Orleans, Miami), and you've got viewers ready to eat popcorn and binge. If Netflix is your jam, look at the "Top 10 Trending," and you're likely to find at least a couple of trial or crime documentaries. Why? Because we are ruled by law and justice in this world.

In God's economy, we have already admitted that we are sinful; therefore, we are all guilty. Every one of us. And yet, directly after the verse I shared with you on Day 1, which declares our guilt (Romans 3:23), we read this passage:

"...and all are justified freely by his grace through the redemption that came by Christ Jesus." Romans 3:24

Justification is to be made right before God. If sin separates us from being in a right relationship with God, His justification, offered to us in a gift of grace, brings us back into right relationship with Him.

But how is this possible? Because, again, we're not righteous. If God is truly all-knowing (omniscient), and He is everywhere at once (omnipresent), then how can we be righteous? Did we somehow get into His blind spot? Is God so busy with other stuff going on in the world that as long as He sees us in church every now and then, we're okay? No, it's bigger than this.

To explain, let me share a metaphor that I heard in one of Pastor Matt Chandler's sermons.[10] He tells us to picture a courtroom, where you and I are the defendants. We know that we are, in fact, guilty. When it is our time to speak, we even stand up and declare our guilt. And yet somehow, when it's decision time, the judge bangs the gavel down and declares us innocent. All charges dropped.

Absolution is the declaration that you have been forgiven. You have been formally released from any guilt, obligation, or punishment. It is the announcement that your sins have been paid for. The debt has been canceled.

In this world, we face a choice. We can receive that declaration of innocence or reject it and receive punishment for our sins. Even worse, we can reject the offer of forgiveness and then try to work our way out of the punishment.

The apostle Paul warns us against this foolishness in Galatians 2:16a: **"We know that a person is not justified by works of the law but through faith in Jesus Christ."**

We are not justified by works of the law, which means at our best we're still lawbreakers. We will not be made right, we will not be declared innocent, simply by behaving in a way that's acceptable before God. The good news is that the banging of the gavel and the declaration of our innocence and forgiveness is not based on whether or not we have been obedient to the law, but by faith in Jesus Christ.

You will not be able to save yourself. You will not be good enough. You will never perfectly fulfill the requirements of the Law. You can't be perfect.

But there is a person who lived a perfect life. He lived a life full of good works and full adherence to the Law. His name is Jesus. Because Jesus was perfect, He was the only one capable of bringing forgiveness of sins to all people. Jesus came into this world on a mission to save sinners by bringing forgiveness to all of those who call on His name.

Without God's forgiveness in our lives, we would never experience freedom in this world. It's impossible. Some people may behave like they are free and look like they are free, but it's a lie. You cannot be free without God declaring you innocent. Jesus came to set all of the oppressed free. He, and He alone, had this special call on His life. And He knew it.

The apostle Paul tells us this so clearly: **"The saying is trustworthy and deserving of full acceptance, that Christ Jesus came into the world to save sinners." 1 Timothy 1:15a (ESV)**

Sin is costly. There are consequences to our bad actions, thoughts, and deeds. And God is not going to let sin go unpunished.

In the Bible, God the Father is often referred to as a judge. We also encounter "judges" all the time in the form of friends, coworkers, and acquaintances who evaluate our actions. But the only judge who matters knows everything about your story. To solve the "sin problem," His answer was to send His Son Jesus into the world on a rescue mission. Amazingly, Jesus took all of the consequences of our sin upon Himself. A sinless man carried the weight of all of your sin, all of my sin, all of humanity's sin—past, present, and future—with Him when He willingly, sacrificially, gave His entire life for us on the cross.

Jesus suffered a brutal death for you. In fact, at the time they didn't have a word to describe the horror and brutality of those who were tortured on a cross, so they came up with a new word: "excruciating." In Latin, this means "out of the cross." Jesus was whipped, beaten, and suffered greatly. Not only this, but He was betrayed by His closest friends. As He was hanging on the cross, struggling to breathe, nearing the end, the Gospel of John says the very last phrase Jesus uttered was one Greek word—*tetelestai*. In English, it is translated: "It is finished."

After this, Jesus bowed His head and gave up His Spirit. Interestingly, the word *tetelestai* was also written on business documents or receipts in New Testament times to indicate that a bill had been paid in full.[11]

TETELESTAI = PAID IN FULL

The devil thought that Jesus was finished. But the only thing that was finished was the payment for our sins.

We owed a debt we could never pay. Jesus paid a debt He did not owe!

The same Spirit that Jesus gave up on Friday would bring resurrection power on Sunday. The resurrection is the objective evidence that the bill has been paid in full. It has been well said that Christ's resurrection is the Father's "Amen" to His Son's declaration, "It is finished." His empty tomb and His resurrection are indisputable testimony that the Father accepted His Son's payment for sin on our behalf.

When Greek readers saw the word *tetelestai*, they would know that what Christ accomplished at the cross was the full payment of all of mankind's sins.

Including yours.

Your sins are no more special than mine. Your sins are not in a different category than mine. Your sins are no greater than mine. And like mine, your sins have been paid in full by the blood of Jesus.

Will you reject this or will you receive this?

Let these words sink in. In fact, go ahead and write your name in the blank below.

_____, YOU ARE FORGIVEN IN THE NAME OF THE FATHER, BY THE BLOOD OF JESUS CHRIST, AND THROUGH THE POWER OF THE HOLY SPIRIT. YOU ARE FORGIVEN.

On Days 20 to 26, you will discover how the sacrifice of Jesus paid in full the consequence of not only Peter's sin, but your sins as well.

RECEIPT

TRANSACTION #19:28

LYING

STEALING

GREED

PRIDE

ENVY

TOTAL:
~~UNPAYABLE~~ TETELESTAI

#FORGIVINGCHALLENGE

DAY 4

RESTORATION

As great as it is to be freed from the consequences of our sin through the absolution of God, His forgiveness extends further than that. Many don't get to experience complete freedom because they stop at absolution. They know that they have been freed from the punishment of their sins and that they are good eternally with God, but many refuse to enter into the next Freedom Phase.

While I was in seminary, I once preached a sermon highlighting freedom. Some of the most daunting, scary sermons I've ever preached were at seminary in front of classmates and professors. After this class was over, the professor graded my sermon. He said, "Zach, you really explained freedom *from* sin well, but as a listener of your message, there's also freedom 'to *something.*' You failed to bring that out. B-minus."

B-minus isn't the worst grade I got at seminary. But I don't want you to come away with a B-minus when it comes to understanding the freedom God is offering you. So, today I'm taking another crack at my professor's advice.

Yesterday's topic of absolution is "freedom from," and today's topic of restoration is "freedom to."

The freedom that God gives you is not only freedom from sin, but freedom to a life of purpose. God's freedom is greater than simply a pardon and release from punishment. He also wants to release you to be a world-changer working alongside Him.

If we go back to Matt Chandler's analogy of the courtroom from yesterday, when the judge declares us innocent, even though we are not, I think all of us breathe a little bit easier. To be declared innocent after our laundry list of sins is shocking. We don't deserve it.

At the same time that this declaration of innocence is happening, we are also fully restored. It's not that you get absolved, and then after a few years of "proving yourself" you are restored into the person God has called you to be. Absolution and restoration happen at the same time.

However, the understanding of restoration seems to unfold more slowly for some people. It's hard to wrap our minds around. If I put my own cards on the table, I don't tend to wrestle with the idea of God paying for my sins. I can see the cross. I know the cross is an aspect of my sin and rebellion. And I know that the sacrifice of Jesus paid for my sins.

Where I struggle is believing that I can still be the person that God has called me to be. I struggle to think that God really enjoys me and could use someone like me because I've woefully failed Him in the past. It's hard *not* to picture Him angry with me after how good He has been to me, and yet I'm still struggling with the same sin that I've told Him over and over I'll never do again.

Restoration hits at identity, and identity is something the enemy loves to attack.

Absolution takes away the guilt. Restoration takes away the shame.

Just as God has fully absolved you, you need to also see that He has fully restored you.

Pastor Timothy Keller writes, "Jesus' salvation is not only like receiving a pardon and release from death row and prison. Then we'd be free, but on our own, left to make our own way in the world, thrown back on our own efforts if we're to make anything of ourselves. But in the Gospel, we discover that Jesus has taken us off death row and then has hung around our neck the Congressional Medal of Honor. We are received and welcomed as heroes, as if we had accomplished extraordinary deeds."[12]

Your past doesn't keep God from using your life in a powerful way. In fact, until you walk in the full restoration that God makes available to you, I don't believe you will fully experience the freedom that God has for you.

You don't just have a just judge, but you have a loving Father as well.

God delights in you like a good father would delight in his son or daughter.

I remember when each of my two sons began to walk. They took two steps, fell down, and we freaked out like they had just won the Olympics! We took videos and sent them to our close friends and family, and then posted them on social media with the hashtag #NextUsainBolt. In the videos, my sons took a few steps, but they also fell flat on their butts. No one who watched the video, including myself, saw my kids take a few steps and thought they were clumsy clowns for falling. We were celebrating the fact that they were walking, however unsteadily.

That's a picture of how God sees you. He cheers you on. He encourages your pursuit. He wants you to hear loud and clearly today that two steps forward and one step backward is still a step forward. So keep stepping. You are moving in the right direction.

Having a loving Father in heaven, who is not only a just judge, changes everything. No offense to any judges out there, but hanging out with a judge just doesn't sound much fun. Judges seem like they would constantly be quoting rules and laws. But hanging out with dad? That sounds fun. I can play golf with my dad. I can watch a ball game with my dad. I can learn from my dad.

God the judge declares you innocent and fully restored into right relationship with Him. Then He bangs the gavel, takes the robes off, and starts hanging out with you.

Your past sins are cast aside, and you are restored into making a difference in this world. This relationship not only means that you are God's son or daughter, but also that you become a co-worker with Him in this world. You get to work for Him and with Him on an eternal mission.

Yesterday you heard the words "I forgive you."

Today, write your name in the blank to complete this sentence from God:
"_____, I love you."

On Days 27 to 33, you will understand that, like Peter, you too are not only absolved of your sin, but restored into a life of meaning and purpose in this world.

DAY 5

SANCTIFICATION

I love the story that my South African friend, Mark, shared with me about a season of his life in which he was dead broke. At the time, he was given a Christmas card from an aunt, who wasn't really known for her great generosity. Thinking it was just a Christmas card, he chucked it in the back seat of his car and drove around with it in his pile of junk for weeks. Meanwhile, he was really struggling to make ends meet and had a very hard several weeks trying to piece his life together, trying to figure out which meal—lunch or dinner—he would eat that day.

Finally, he was cleaning out the back seat of his car one day, and he found this unopened Christmas card. When he opened it at last, he found a significant amount of money that his aunt had given to him to help him get through his financial ordeal. All along, he had been sitting on a gift of financial freedom but still living in financial bondage. The gift had been there, but he didn't receive it. He didn't open it and live out the freedom that the gift provided.

It is possible to have the full gift of our sins forgiven and the full restoration of our identity through Jesus's sacrifice and still not live in freedom. Don't hear me wrong: Jesus has done all the hard work for you! But until you open the gift and live out the freedom that the gift provides, you will stay in a sort of bondage. Jesus didn't give you absolution and restoration so that you wouldn't do anything with it.

He gave you absolution and restoration so that you would enjoy those gifts. Not just eternally, but here, right now. Freedom isn't only available in heaven. It's available for you to experience now.

You do not experience freedom in this world until you step into a life of sanctification.

Sanctification, by definition, is the process of being freed from sin, or being purified or made holy. Sanctification is, by the way, a lifelong process. While absolution and restoration will never be things that we can do, sanctification is a process that we work on, in conjunction with God, for the rest of our lives. It's never perfect and never complete, but when we participate with God in this process, freedom truly is experienced.

While each one of us is called and restored back into a life of purpose through God's grace, the path of sanctification often gives us a second chance in an area in which we previously failed. From an eternal perspective, we'll never right our wrongs because Jesus did that for us, but I am most fascinated by how God oftentimes will bring meaning and purpose into our lives from some of the worst parts of our stories.

Our greatest stumbles produce our greatest stories.

That's why some of the most successful addiction counselors were at one point addicted to drugs themselves. In fact, a key part of recovery through Alcoholics Anonymous is the 12th and final step. Check it out: "Having had a spiritual awakening as the result of these Steps, we tried to carry this message to alcoholics, and to practice these principles in all our affairs."[13] The final step to full freedom is taking the thing that was against you and using it to help bring freedom to others.

God rescued you so that you could help rescue others!

Are there any sins, any scars from those sins, that God wants to use through you to help free others?

Sin is the most powerful weapon that the devil throws at us in this world. But when we walk in true freedom, God can take the weapon that was meant to destroy you and turn it into a weapon that not only brings purpose to your life, but brings freedom and salvation to others.

The body of Jesus was nailed onto an instrument of death called a cross. The cross, which the enemy used to kill Jesus, would eventually become the symbol of our victory. Jesus used the enemy's weapon to destroy the enemy and bring freedom to all of us!

God has a degree in bringing deliverance out of destruction.

This is what Jesus did for us, and this is the opportunity we are offered today! Total freedom comes when we take the former sins that have been against us, oppressing us and slowing us down, and give them over to God. Not only do we experience God's forgiveness, but He then puts us in a place to use our lives and tell our stories. We are able to do this with and through the power of Jesus!

The SCARS process is not always simple. It's usually ugly, and it will leave a mark. But your scars can help tell the beautiful story of Jesus. Mike Foster writes, "Too many of us believe the lie that we need to sanitize our scandals, brush away our grief, and cover up our scars."[14] Sanctification is an opportunity for God to work through your scars to help bring freedom to others.

Every scar tells a story. When you tell your story of how Jesus brought grace into your life, you end up bringing freedom to others. This is what the apostle John reminds us in Revelation 12:11a: **"They triumphed over him [Satan] by the blood of the Lamb and by the word of their testimony."**

The "blood of the Lamb" is the blood that Jesus shed for us on the cross. He is known as "The Lamb of God" all throughout the Bible. John reminds us that the power of our stories, rooted in THE story of Jesus, will bring ultimate freedom and victory over our enemy.

THE BLOOD OF JESUS + OUR STORY > THE DEVIL

I want you to know that God has chosen you and filled you with His Spirit to make a difference in this world. In a world filled with division, unforgiveness, and bitterness, we are the forgiven sons and daughters of God, and we have the opportunity to bring freedom to others just as God has brought freedom to us.

Imagine how the world might change if we truly walked in the power of God's freedom.

Sanctification is the opportunity for you to be fully free. Be free and tell your story!

On Days 34 to 40, you will be given the opportunity, like Peter, to be completely free from your sin, and in response, to live a holy life pursuing Jesus and bringing the freedom you've experienced to others.

S.C.A.R.S.

SIN

DAY 6

SNUB-NOSED TO BIG BOULDER

Make no mistake about it: The Bible is all about Jesus. The story of Jesus as Savior of the World frames the entire book from Genesis to Revelation. Inside the pages of the Bible, Jesus offers not just an invitation to be saved by Him, but to walk with Him and let Him be the Lord of our lives today. One of those invitations was very clearly given to a man named Peter.

You could argue that Peter is the only other fully formed character in the Gospels besides Jesus. He is listed first chronologically in any story that mentions the disciples, and he is mentioned more than five times the number of any other disciple. "He is referred to almost 200 times in the New Testament. The disciple John is mentioned only 31 times," says Michael Card in *A Fragile Stone*.[15] He also plays the most vital role in the first twelve chapters of Acts.

This week, we will be introduced to the disciple Peter, and to a series of big blunders by which many define his life. I believe the story of forgiveness that Jesus will offer to Peter is the most personal and relational story of forgiveness in all of the Bible. While Jesus is the hero of the Bible, Peter serves "as a 'foil' to Jesus," says Adam Hamilton, a pastor and author. "A foil is a supporting character whose part contrasts, highlights, and even exalts the qualities of the lead character... Just as Jesus reveals and represents God, Peter represents all who seek to follow Jesus."[16]

My hope is that as we examine this story of forgiveness, you will begin to see yourself in the character of Peter. As you watch Jesus so amazingly give grace to him, my hope is that you too would know that Jesus offers grace to you—and that not only would you receive this grace, but, like Peter, you will learn to walk in it and be fully transformed by it.

If you ever visit New Zealand, you might choose to stop by a hill on the North Island called Taumatawhakatangihangakoauauotamateaturipukakapikimaunga-horonukupokaiwhenuakitanatahu. No joke. If that's too much of a mouthful, the short form is Taumatawhakatangihangakoauauotamateapokaiwhenuakitanatahu. It is listed in the Guinness World Records as the longest official place name in the world.

The name means: "The summit where Tamatea, the man with the big knees, the climber of mountains, the land-swallower who travelled about, played his nose flute to his loved one."[17] As strange as this name is, it's quite biblical. A name in the Bible is often a description of the person himself or herself—or what the parents would like their child to become.[18]

Names are significant, and every now and then in the Bible, God changes someone's name. This is important to know because when we are first introduced to the biblical character known as Peter, he has a different name: Simon. At the time, Simon is fishing on a boat because fishing was the family business. This was his future before Jesus met him.

The very first recorded words that Jesus speaks to Peter are found in John 1:42: **"'You are Simon son of John. You will be called Cephas' (which, when translated is Peter)."**

Peter starts as Simon, but Jesus immediately declares that he will now be Peter, even though he hasn't done anything to earn a new name. Interestingly, the name Simon is a Greek nickname that means "snub-nosed." More commonly, Simon was a derivative of Simeon, which means, "God has heard." The name that Jesus gives to Simon is Peter, which means "the rock, or big boulder."

I like that Jesus changed his name *before* Peter ever did anything to earn it. Oftentimes, we get it wrong by thinking that God will only love us, accept us, forgive us, and ultimately free us if we first prove to Him that we are worthy of His love and acceptance. Even after his name is changed to Peter, if you look into his life as portrayed in the Gospels, Peter did not live up to his new name many times. You could argue that you see a lot more "big blunder" in Peter than you do "big boulder."

In *Simon Peter: Flawed but Faithful Disciple*, Pastor Adam Hamilton says, "How could Jesus call Simon a rock? After all, this man is going to blow it consistently. He will be less like a rock and more like a reed or blade of grass, easily moved, swayed, or broken. He will miss the point again and again."[19]

Even after receiving grace and a new identity in Jesus, there are still times we fail to live up to the name that God places on us. And yet, He still calls us by our new name.

This is what God does. He comes into our stories and invites us into a new calling. He gives us a new identity. He declares that who you are and who you've been doesn't have to follow you into the future. When God changes someone's name, it's because He's calling him or her to live out a new mission or new identity in this world. Jesus saw some great potential in Peter. Everyone else saw Simon the snub-nosed, but Jesus saw Peter the rock. Through this name, He gave Peter a vision of what God sees in Him.

Just as God saw something in Peter, He sees something in you too. Jesus sees in you what you can be—regardless of what you've done or what other people have said about you. God loves you for who you are, but His love doesn't leave you just as you are. He desires you to step into the identity that He's won for you by His grace.

You might think that you are not special enough for Jesus to call someone like you. Even if Peter didn't do anything of note to receive this new identity, certainly He was chosen because of his place in this world, right? Wrong. The more you look into Peter's story before he met Jesus, the more you see that there really wasn't much that stood out.

In the Jewish population, there was a class of people, going back hundreds of years before the time of Jesus and Peter, called *am ha'arertz*. The phrase literally means "the people of the land." The term has a complicated history, but according to Adam Hamilton's *Simon Peter: Flawed but Faithful Disciple*, "by the time of Simon Peter it meant people who were poor, uneducated, lower class, and particularly people who were not careful in their observance of the Law."[20]

In addition, Acts 4:13 describes Peter (and his disciple friend John) as unschooled and ordinary men. And yet, through this ordinary, unschooled man, we have a person who would become the right-hand man of Jesus.

After Jesus called Peter to be His disciple, the text says that immediately Peter followed Him. This was the sort of guy that Peter was. All in. Peter became the outspoken leader of the disciples. He was a natural-born leader who was never afraid to speak his mind or to make a bold move. In fact, Peter was the only disciple who had the courage to jump out of the boat and walk on water toward Jesus, even with a wild wind buffeting their vessel. You could make the case that he was one of Jesus's best friends in the whole world.

In the midst of so many great actions, moments, and words, and with so much done for him and entrusted to him by Jesus, the big boulder, however, is most known for a series of three big blunders. Peter would fail Jesus miserably.

The story of Peter and Jesus is significant for you and me, because much like Peter, we've been given a new name and identity in Jesus. And yet despite all that He's done for us, we still fall woefully short of God's expectations. In *Forgiving Challenge*, we will discover that even though we continue to miss the mark, God will relentlessly pursue us, just as He pursued Peter. If Jesus can forgive someone like Peter for what he did, He can forgive you too!

So what sin did Peter commit? We'll find that out on Day 7.

CHALLENGE

WHAT'S YOUR NAME?

Do you know why your name was chosen?

_____

_____

What does your given name mean?

_____

_____

Do you live up to your name or fall short of your name?

_____

_____

What name(s), or identity(ies), do you currently carry that are most important/ significant for you? Explain.

_____

_____

Is there a particular name(s) that you long to hear someone call you? Explain.

_____

_____

6/40

DAY 7

BIG BOULDER OR BIG BLUNDER?

One of the pivotal moments in Peter's life—and the life of the church—occurred in Caesarea Philippi at the base of Mount Hermon. As tensions were rising quickly between Jesus and the Jewish leaders of the day, Jesus took the disciples aside in Matthew 16:13-19:

"When Jesus came to the region of Caesarea Philippi, he asked his disciples, 'Who do people say the Son of Man is?'

"They replied, 'Some say John the Baptist; others say Elijah; and still others, Jeremiah or one of the prophets.'

"'But what about you?' he asked. 'Who do you say I am?'

"Simon Peter answered, 'You are the Messiah, the Son of the living God.'

"Jesus replied, 'Blessed are you, Simon son of Jonah, for this was not revealed to you by flesh and blood, but by my Father in heaven. And I tell you that you are Peter, and on this rock, I will build my church, and the gates of Hades will not overcome it. I will give you the keys of the kingdom of heaven; whatever you bind on earth will be bound in heaven, and whatever you loose on earth will be loosed in heaven.'"

Peter gets it so right in this exchange! He declares, "You are the Messiah, the Son of the living God." Then Jesus assures Peter that the church will be founded on this confession. What's more, Peter is given a special position reserved for only one person. Jesus anoints him to take the perennial leadership role in the establishment of the church. He will be the very first pastor of God's church.

Wow! What a call placed on the life of Peter!

Don't miss an important fact here as well. This anointing of Peter in Caesarea Philippi takes place *in front of dramatic rock formations—literal big boulders.* There, Jesus doubles down and tells Peter that he is the Lord's big boulder. In addition, if you go to the place in Caesarea Philippi where it is believed that Jesus and the disciples had this interaction, you'll find a large cave. Pagans at the time believed the cave led directly down to Hades, the underworld. This location gave extra power to Jesus's statement that the gates of Hades will not overcome His church built upon this rock.

With all of this happening in the background, Jesus would soon be sitting around a table, eating the Last Supper with His disciples. Not only does Jesus declare that one of the twelve disciples will betray Him, leading to His crucifixion, but another disciple will deny Him. Peter stands up boldly and declares:

"Even if all fall away on account of you, I never will." Matthew 26:33

Peter is not afraid to be outspoken. But even in his bold statement, he found a way to be offensive to the others in the room. He essentially said that he will never stoop to denying Jesus, even if everyone else in the room does. But Jesus answers back:

"'Truly I tell you, this very night, before the rooster crows, you will disown me three times.'
"But Peter declared, 'Even if I have to die with you, I will never disown you.' And all the other disciples said the same." Matthew 26:34-35

It's interesting that the phrase "all the other disciples said the same" is recorded. Very rarely do we ever talk about the denials and dis-ownings of the other disciples.

And yet, Peter comes into focus here because he is the outspoken leader of the disciples. As a leader, you typically have more attention on you. You get too much credit in the good times and too much blame in the bad times.

It turns out that Jesus's prediction would come true. Here's the story in Luke 22:54-62:

> **"Then seizing him [Jesus], they led him away and took him into the house of the high priest. Peter followed at a distance. And when some there had kindled a fire in the middle of the courtyard and had sat down together, Peter sat down with them. A servant girl saw him seated there in the firelight. She looked closely at him and said, 'This man was with him.'**
>
> **"But he denied it. 'Woman, I don't know him,' he said.**
>
> **"A little later someone else saw him and said, 'You also are one of them.'**
>
> **"'Man, I am not!' Peter replied.**
>
> **"About an hour later another asserted, 'Certainly this fellow was with him, for he is a Galilean.'**
>
> **"Peter replied, 'Man, I don't know what you're talking about!' Just as he was speaking, the rooster crowed. The Lord turned and looked straight at Peter. Then Peter remembered the word the Lord had spoken to him: 'Before the rooster crows today, you will disown me three times.' And he went outside and wept bitterly."**

Peter, the rock, Jesus's right-hand man, flat-out denied Jesus at a time when the Lord needed him most. Peter badly fell short of what Jesus had taught him.

What's striking to me is Peter's lack of courage. Peter was the one who jumped out of the boat, cut off a servant's ear, and made bold proclamations. You get the feeling that he was able to stand up to anyone and anything. And yet here he is, at his first denial, crumbling in front of one little servant girl.

Sometimes, even with the best of intentions, the weight of this world falls upon us. Sadly, we make decisions that in the moment may feel good or safe, but eventually leave us feeling empty. Sin does just that. It usually feels good in the moment, but we're empty afterward. The good news of Jesus is that even after we have sinned and experience the feeling of emptiness, He comes to us and offers us a second, third, and infinite chances.

For as much good as Peter has done in his life, he is "nearly always portrayed as a flawed disciple—one who seeks to follow Jesus, yet one who is also confused, afraid, and faltering," writes Adam Hamilton.[21]

This is quite different from the normal patterns in history. Typically, a beloved character's flaws are minimized and forgotten as stories of their heroic acts are remembered and embellished. Not so for Peter. Even though Peter certainly had a lifetime filled with more achievements than nearly any other human could boast, the story that Peter is most known for is his denials of Jesus. It was a series of bad mistakes that forever is equated with him. At a time when his friend, his Savior, his Teacher, his Lord needed his faithfulness most, he denied Jesus. Not just once. Not twice. But three times.

Like Peter, God has entrusted much to us, but we've fallen short of what He's asked of us, and who He's called us to be.

You'd think that failing Jesus like this would be the end of the story. Far from it.

Any failure is an opportunity to fall into the grace and forgiveness of Jesus.

WRITE YOUR FUNERAL EULOGY

History remembers Peter in different ways. One of the themes of *Forgiving Challenge* is that each of us tells a story with our lives. You do too. It may be a bit morbid to think about, but if you had to write your own funeral eulogy today, what would you say about yourself? How would you be remembered up to this point? Later in *Forgiving Challenge*, we'll give you an opportunity to write about what our future chapters might look like, but today simply tell your story up to this point.

Here is the typical eulogy structure with questions that could guide you:[22]

- Begin with opening remarks. (Typically, this would include your relationship to the deceased.)

- What made the deceased special or unique (his/her hobbies or interests)?

- If the deceased was religious, talk about his/her commitment to faith.

- Was the deceased a role model? If so, give personal or general examples.

- What contribution or mark did the deceased make in those closest to him/her and/or to the outside world?

- How will the deceased be remembered?

- Offer words of comfort and perhaps a final farewell in closing.

IN LOVING MEMORY OF

_____
(your name)

_____

_____

_____

_____

_____

_____

_____

_____

7/40

DAY 8

BIG DEAL OR NO BIG DEAL?

It's easy in the world in which we live to either minimize sin or elevate sin: to think it's not a big deal or a *really* big deal. Or perhaps certain categories of sin are a big deal but others are not.

Here's the truth. Sin, no matter what type or how "big" you think it is, is a very big deal. God hates all that is wicked; therefore, He hates sin.

At the same time, God loves the entire created world. Heaven will be a full restoration of this world, but His most prized possession is you and me. Look at what James, Jesus's brother, had to say about how we fit into God's full creation:

> **"Whatever is good and perfect is a gift coming down to us from God our Father, who created all the lights in the heavens. He never changes or casts a shifting shadow. He chose to give birth to us by giving us his true word. And we, out of all creation, became his prized possession."**
> **James 1:17-19 (NLT)**

James reminds us that God created all things, but we are the apple of His eye.

When someone loves you so much, it feels awful to fall short of their hopes for you. I think that's why I resonate so much with the sin of Peter. He had been entrusted much and had a front-row seat to the teachings, healings, and miracles of Jesus, and yet he still failed miserably. He had no excuses.

Just as God loved, entrusted, and equipped Peter, He has done the same for you and me. And yet, like Peter, we too have failed. We have no excuses.

As I said on Day 1, any missing of the mark is sin. Little misses still come with big consequences. We see this principle in action in many areas of our life. A throw from a quarterback to a receiver may be off by only an inch, but that inch could be the difference between a touchdown or an interception. Where you hit the head pin in bowling could mean the difference between a strike or a split.

God hates sin of all magnitude because it separates us from a relationship with Him.

The prophet Isaiah reminds us of this: **"But your iniquities have separated you from your God; your sins have hidden his face from you, so that he will not hear." Isaiah 59:2**

Our culture's narrative, which is being forced upon us, is that we are to affirm one another for who we are. As I stated on Day 1, this is a dangerous lie that many Christians not only believe, but are spreading as well.

The problem, of course, is that not all who live in this world follow the standards of God. We ought not expect those who haven't signed up to follow Jesus as Lord to live by the same standards to which we are called. I can understand why those who don't follow Jesus would want to reject today's devotion, but those who follow Jesus should have no problem whatsoever recognizing that each and every one of us is not a perfect person.

With imperfection comes great consequence. Sin removes the very thing that God ultimately desires: relationship with Him. Paul reminds his protégé Timothy of this truth. As he writes in 1 Timothy 2:4, **"God wants all people to be saved and to come to a knowledge of the truth."**

So, in this sense, sin is a very big deal. We ought never minimize sin and its effects.

We also don't need to elevate sin beyond what it is. For this fact also remains: As great as sin is, God's grace is greater.

In fact, in the verse just prior to the one from Isaiah quoted on page 59, the prophet reminds us: **"Surely the arm of the Lord is not too short to save, nor his ear too dull to hear." Isaiah 59:1**

Even though sin separates us from Him, because of His power and through His grace, our sins do not leave us without hope. I've met many people who aren't living a life of freedom because, while they believe God can forgive others, they have a hard time believing God can forgive someone like them. But this is a lie. You, and all of your sins, were fully paid for by Jesus Christ.

Knowing Peter's full story makes the words that Peter writes in the Bible come to life even more. 1 Peter 4:8b says: **"Love covers over a multitude of sins."**

Our love, through the power of the Holy Spirit inside of us, can help bring people to relationship with God, but it was ultimately God's love, displayed on the cross, that covered the multitude of sins that we heaped upon Jesus. I can just imagine Peter as he's writing these words remembering the grace of God in his life for all of his big blunders.

The tension we face in this world is not to minimize sin and also not to minimize grace.

We must call out sin and talk about its consequences. It absolutely has to be dealt with, which is why we're spending considerable time understanding the seriousness of sin. At the same time, we must also comprehend the greatness of God's grace.

Sin is a big deal. But God's grace is a bigger deal.

ELEVATOR OR MINIMIZER?

Do you naturally tend to elevate sin or minimize sin? Why?

_____

Are there certain sins you *elevate* over other sins? Explain.

_____

Are there certain sins you *minimize* over other sins? Explain.

_____

Are there certain personal sins that you feel more guilt about than others? Explain.

_____

_____

Is it appropriate to feel more guilt about some sins than others?

_____

_____

8/40

DAY 9

LAW AND GOSPEL

The path to freedom is not without pain. The last few days, we've laid the groundwork for the idea of sin, but today I want to begin the process of identifying specific sins in our lives. As painful as this part of the freedom process is, it's important that we look backward before we take steps forward.

Freedom begins by acknowledging what we need freedom from.

One of the main ways I have been taught to read the Bible is through the lens of Law and Gospel. Martin Chemnitz notes the difference between the Law and Gospel in his *Formula of Concord*: "Everything that proclaims something about our sin and God's wrath is the proclamation of the law, however and whenever it may take place. On the other hand, the Gospel is the kind of proclamation that points to and bestows nothing else than grace and forgiveness in Jesus."[23]

These contrasting messages of Law and Gospel are evident throughout the Bible, and sometimes they land right next to one another. We learned about Romans 3:23-24 on Day 3. These two verses are a great example of Law and Gospel right next to each other. First, check out the Law from Romans 3:23:

"For all have sinned and fall short of the glory of God."

The apostle Paul then lays out Gospel in the very next verse in Romans 3:24:

"...and all are justified freely by his grace through the redemption that came by Christ Jesus."

God uses the Law to expose the depth of how far we've fallen. He uses the Gospel to rescue us out of the depths and bring us to new heights.

Our natural sinful condition, however, will try to turn the Law into something that it is not. Whenever we give too much power to the Law and use it to save ourselves, we walk in further bondage. This sort of thinking, though, is quite natural and found in every other major religion: "What do I need to do for God to love me?" But God's love cannot be earned by our strict adherence and obedience to the Law. The purpose of the Law, therefore, is to bring us to our knees and put us in a place where we are ready to receive the Gospel.

The path to healing and ultimate freedom begins by sharing our struggles in order to receive God's grace. Before we accept God's grace, we must first accept our need for it.

It may not be fun talking about the parts of our individual stories where we've fallen. We all have things we'd rather not share. Today begins the journey of learning to talk about those things, so that we can allow God's grace to enter into our stories. God is not afraid of your story. He is not surprised by your story. He will not distance Himself from you because of your story. He asks that you simply come to Him with your story, so that He can make you whole and begin a new chapter for you.

Are you ready?

Many of you reading this carry deep wounds and scars from sins that you still think about today. For some of you, a particular sin may be haunting you from years ago. Perhaps you made a decision that you never thought you were capable of. For others, it might be something that started out rather small, but over time has grown into a full-on addiction that you can't get past.

So what sins are you carrying? What personal scars have you suffered in your life?

In the Ten Commandments alone, found in Exodus 20, if we answer truthfully, all of us would see the need for God's forgiveness.

Have you ever placed anything before our God? Have you ever had a problem with idolatry? While our nation may not struggle with literal handmade "idols" like the ones in the Old Testament, any time we place anyone or anything above God, that is considered an idol.

Have you ever taken God's name in vain, neglected the Sabbath, or dishonored your father or mother?

Have you ever killed, committed adultery, stolen, lied, or coveted anything or anyone?

Jesus took it further in the Sermon on the Mount and made our perfect adherence to the Law even harder. He reminded us that it's not only about keeping the letter of the Law prescribed by the Ten Commandments, but also upholding the spirit of the Law.

He would say things like this in Matthew 5:21-22a: **"You have heard that it was** said to the people long ago, 'You shall not murder, and anyone who murders will be subject to judgment.' But I tell you that anyone who is angry with a brother or sister will be subject to judgment."

Even if you haven't physically murdered someone, but you have anger in your heart toward them, Jesus claims that you are guilty of breaking the Law. Or how about this one, just a few verses later? In Matthew 5:27-28, Jesus says: **"You have heard that it was said, 'You shall not commit adultery.' But I tell you that anyone who looks at a woman lustfully has already committed adultery with her in his heart."**

What does all of this mean? It means you are guilty!

Rather than trying to fake it until you make it, and act like you have everything perfectly put together in this world, the first step in freedom is admitting that you don't. This freedom comes when we bring all of the worst parts of our stories to a God who is capable of healing us.

In his book *Freeway*, Mike Foster says, "For it is the dings, the skinned knees, and the broken bones of life that Jesus is most interested in. Whether we like it or not, pain is part of life, and our divine rescuer doesn't bring a small box of Band-Aids or a couple of Advil. He brings supernatural healing, and if you and I are being honest, healing is exactly what we need right now."[24]

Healing is offered in Jesus. Today, let's admit our need for it.

CHALLENGE

THE SIN TEST

Take the following sin test, adapted from one created by Flatirons Community Church in Denver, Colorado.[25] Mark "Yes" or "No" next to each question.

1. Have you ever lusted after something or someone that wasn't yours? _____

2. Do you have anything in your life that you regret? _____

3. Do you have anything in your life that you are constantly ashamed of? _____

4. Have you ever cut yourself or intentionally harmed yourself? _____

5. Have you ever physically, verbally, or sexually abused someone else? _____

6. Have you ever abused drugs or alcohol? _____

7. Have you ever thought about or attempted suicide? _____

8. Have you ever had a sexual relationship outside of marriage? _____

9. Do you have any secrets that you've never shared with anyone? _____

10. Are you doing anything wrong that you can't quit? _____

11. Have you purposefully and willingly viewed pornography? _____

12. Have you ever lied to someone in your effort to hide your actions? _____

What emotions are you experiencing right now?

_____

_____

_____

_____

_____

The point of the Law is to bring you to a place to receive the Gospel. Read these verses and choose one to commit to memory today.

2 Corinthians 12:9: **"'My grace is sufficient for you, for my power is made perfect in weakness.' Therefore, I will boast all the more gladly about my weaknesses, so that Christ's power may rest on me."**

Ephesians 2:8-9: **"For it is by grace you have been saved, through faith—and this is not from yourselves, it is the gift of God—not by works, so that no one can boast."**

Romans 5:8: **"But God demonstrates his own love for us in this: While we were still sinners, Christ died for us."**

Which verse will you memorize? Start by writing it down on the lines below:

_____

_____

_____

9/40

DAY 10

THE GREAT OMISSION

One of the most popular television shows of all time was *Seinfeld*. Predictably, after a long run of success, it's always difficult to please the critics and fanbase in a series finale. The finale of *Seinfeld* left many disappointed, even outraged. I remember one prominent analyst giving the finale ½ star out of 4.

One of the major complaints about the finale was that all four main characters, Jerry, George, Elaine, and Kramer, were arrested. Instead of intervening in a carjacking situation, the four ridiculed and mocked the victim and, essentially, they were arrested for not doing something.

Yesterday, we spent time considering sins that we have committed. But there is another type of sin that often goes unnoticed and doesn't get dealt with—sins of omission.

Omission, of course, is a failure to do something.

Interestingly, the main characters in *Seinfeld* were thrown into jail for breaking the town's *Good Samaritan* Law. The name of this law, of course, comes from one of Jesus's most famous parables. A parable is simply a story meant to illustrate a point. Let's read this parable in Luke 10:25-28 to find the main point:

"On one occasion an expert in the law stood up to test Jesus. 'Teacher,' he asked, 'what must I do to inherit eternal life?'

> **"'What is written in the Law?'** he replied. **'How do you read it?'**
>
> **"He answered, '"Love the Lord your God with all your heart and with all your soul and with all your strength and with all your mind"; and, "Love your neighbor as yourself."'**
>
> **"'You have answered correctly,'** Jesus replied. **'Do this and you will live.'"**

Jesus is talking primarily to a Jewish audience, and the one who addressed Him is, in fact, a Jewish expert in the Law. The expert knows the commandments we discussed yesterday. He even recites the correct summary of all of the laws.

> **"But he wanted to justify himself, so he asked Jesus, 'And who is my neighbor?'" Luke 10:29**

The Jews in the day of Jesus were taught to love their neighbor, but they were also taught to hate their enemy. In this particular case, the man wants to test Jesus; he wants Jesus to specify the boundaries that distinguish who qualifies as a neighbor. That way, he will know if, in fact, he has perfectly held to the Law.

This is the way many of us approach God. We want to know exactly what to do, what God expects of us, because we are determined to try to check the right boxes. Rather than giving specific boundaries, though, Jesus is about to expand this Jewish leader's mindset. Let's see what Jesus said:

> **"A man was going down from Jerusalem to Jericho, when he was attacked by robbers. They stripped him of his clothes, beat him and went away, leaving him half dead. A priest happened to be going down the same road, and when he saw the man, he passed by on the other side. So too, a Levite, when he came to the place and saw him, passed by on the**

other side. But a Samaritan, as he traveled, came where the man was; and when he saw him, he took pity on him. He went to him and bandaged his wounds, pouring on oil and wine. Then he put the man on his own donkey, brought him to an inn and took care of him. The next day he took out two denarii and gave them to the innkeeper. 'Look after him,' he said, 'and when I return, I will reimburse you for any extra expense you may have.'"
Luke 10:30-35

In this scenario, we have a man hurting on the side of the road, and he is treated unjustly. A religious man, a priest, comes by first and completely ignores him. A Levite, another category of religious official, also passes by, completely ignoring him. But it was the third person, a Samaritan, who helped this man.

It's important to understand that Jews hated Samaritans, whom they viewed as tainted for intermarrying with Gentiles. Likely, the fact that the Samaritan man was the hero of the parable shocked the audience and the expert in the Law. Jesus destroyed the boundaries that the Jewish people had established. He continues:

> **"'Which of these three do you think was a neighbor to the man who fell into the hands of robbers?'**
> **"The expert in the law replied, 'The one who had mercy on him.'**
> **"Jesus told him, 'Go and do likewise.'" Luke 10:36-37**

Note that the expert of the Law couldn't even say the name "Samaritan." Instead, he said, "The one…"

The main point of the parable is that when we have an opportunity to help others and battle the injustices of this world, we are called to do so. Even if the "other" person in the story isn't technically your neighbor or your ethnicity, when you see someone in need, God invites you into this opportunity to help. When you do not step into the opportunities to help that God puts in front of you, that is, in fact, a sin.

One of my favorite all-time theologians is Dallas Willard, and one of my favorite books of his is *The Great Omission*. Willard says, "The last command Jesus gave the church before He ascended to heaven was the Great Commission, the call for Christians to 'make disciples of all nations.' But Christians have responded by making 'Christians,' not 'disciples.'"[26] Willard defines a disciple as person who has decided that the most important thing in life is "to learn how to do what Jesus said to do."

Many of us read the Bible and the commands of God—especially the commands that tell us what we are called to do—as suggestions. The clarion call of Jesus to His disciples is to go and make other disciples. Any pursuit of Jesus without making disciples falls short and misses the mark of what Jesus has asked. And remember, what is missing the mark called? Sin.

When I think of someone who racked up a resume more impressive than perhaps any other disciple of Jesus ever, I think of the apostle Paul. That's why this statement of his shocks me:

> **"Here is a trustworthy saying that deserves full acceptance: Christ Jesus came into the world to save sinners—of whom I am the worst."**
> **1 Timothy 1:15**

Is this just false humility from Paul?

Even if you somehow still feel pretty good about your overall performance after yesterday's sin test, I believe Paul is telling us that the closer we get to Jesus, the more we see how truly broken we are. Even if we eliminate from our lives a lot of the things God calls us not to do, there is another category of things God calls us to do. We have so much to do.

The more I pursue Jesus and the closer I get to Him, the more I realize that I haven't done much of what God has called me to do. For those of us who have followed Jesus for decades, it could be that sins of omission may be more damning than sins of commission.

In reality, if we are to perfectly hold up to the Law, we must do each and every one of the commands of God. James, the brother of Jesus, reminds us of this truth in James 2:10: **"For whoever keeps the whole law and yet stumbles at just one point is guilty of breaking it all."**

This is why any pursuit of perfection and checking all the right boxes will always lead to disastrous results. Rather than fighting and clinging to our innocence, let us admit that we are, in fact, sinful. We are sinful in things that we have done and things we have not done.

CHALLENGE

THE OMISSION TEST

Take the following omission test. Below are ten things God has commanded us to do. Mark "Yes" or "No" if you've been actively involved in these over the past month.

1. Take care of the widow. (James 1:27, Isaiah 1:17) _____

2. Take care of the orphan. (James 1:27) _____

3. Feed the hungry. (Matthew 25:35) _____

4. Invite/befriend a stranger. (Matthew 25:35) _____

5. Clothe the naked. (Matthew 25:36) _____

6. Visit the sick. (Matthew 25:36) _____

7. Visit the imprisoned. (Matthew 25:36) _____

8. Defend the rights of the defenseless. (Proverbs 31:8-9) _____

9. Pray for those who mistreat you. (Matthew 5:44) _____

10. Go and make disciples. (Matthew 28:18-20) _____

What emotions are you experiencing right now?

_____

Pick one of the ten commands above and act on it in a tangible way today.

10/40

DAY 11

KILLING SPIDERS AND LAMBS

Did you know that the number one phobia that people have today is arachnophobia, or the fear of spiders?[27]

Living in Florida for the past decade, we have seen our share of impressive wildlife. Florida is most known for alligators, black bears, sharks, and jellyfish, but it is another creature that consistently ranks among the deadliest in the state: the brown recluse spider.

The recluse spider is known to play dead when threatened, only to pounce on you with a bite that could vary in intensity from no effects all the way to death. This species of spider thrives in warmer climates and blends in pretty well with its surroundings. The most common places where recluse spiders show up are in clothing you haven't worn for a long time. So inspect your clothing before bundling-up or wear gloves when reaching in for that old sweater.

When it comes to spiders, a lot of us operate with a "kill or be killed" mentality.

In the book *Kill the Spider*, Carlos Whittaker recalls when his dad, Pastor Fermin, was holding a three-day revival in Panama. At the end of the first day, a woman, Ms. Ramirez, came up to receive prayer. She asked that God would clean all of the cobwebs out of her life. Pastor Fermin prayed this prayer faithfully over her. "God, clean the cobwebs out of her life." On night two, the woman asked for the same prayer even more confidently. Carlos's father prayed even more fervently. "God, clean the cobwebs out of her life." Finally, on the third day, Ms. Ramirez came up and again pleaded one last time to pray that God would clean the cobwebs out of her life. At this point, Pastor Fermin stopped her mid-sentence, realizing they were praying the wrong prayer.

He then said, "Father, we do not ask you tonight to clean the cobwebs from Ms. Ramirez's life. In fact, Lord, keep them there for now. But tonight, we ask for something greater. Tonight, we ask that you KILL THE SPIDER in Ms. Ramirez's life. In the name of Jesus, I pray. Amen."[28]

Many of us have become experts in cleaning and focusing on the cobwebs in our lives. Some of us have learned not only how to live, but how to have success in this world, in spite of our failures and mistakes. We've performed fairly well with cobwebs all around us. The problem with managing cobwebs is we never get to the root issue of it all: the spider.

Many of us go about our lives today like the couch sitting in our living room. On the outside, the couch appears just fine—clean and tidy. But underneath the cushions lies all kinds of junk. A life in which we look good on the outside but are wasting away on the inside is not the free and abundant life that God wants for us. In Matthew 23:27-28, Jesus drives home this very point when He compares the Pharisees to whitewashed tombs, **"which look beautiful on the outside but on the inside are full of the bones of the dead and everything unclean."** If all we ever do is stuff away or suppress the worst parts of our stories, we'll never be fully free.

In 1 Samuel 16:7b (ESV), God reminds the prophet Samuel: **"For the Lord sees not as man sees: man looks on the outward appearance, but the Lord looks on the heart."**

God isn't interested in cleaning up your life only on the outside. God is interested in the complete removal and destruction of sin in your life. To be made alive in Him requires that a part of you must first die. We cannot have a free and abundant life outside of the presence of God. The problem, however, is that nothing unholy or unclean can be in the presence of a holy God. Habakkuk 1:13a says that God's eyes **"are too pure to look on evil."** God tolerates no sin.

To show you the magnitude of this truth, we need only look to the covenant that God cut with His people in the Old Testament. God laid out a rigorous, precise, and careful plan to atone for the sins of the Israelite people. Once a year, known as the Day of Atonement, the High Priest of Israel would enter into a perfectly constructed, cube-shape, windowless room known as the "Holy of Holies." Inside the Holy of Holies was the Ark of the Covenant, which symbolized Israel's special relationship with God. On this particular day, the high priest would burn incense and sprinkle the blood of a sacrificial animal on the mercy seat of the Ark of the Covenant. By doing so, the high priest would atone for his own sins and those of the Israelite people.

It wasn't a spider that was killed for the sins of the people, but instead an innocent, spotless lamb.

On the outside of the Holy of Holies was a massive, 30-foot-wide by 30-foot-tall veil made of fine linen and yarn that separated this room from the rest of the temple. This large veil was used as a barrier between man and God. The only one allowed access into this room, the Israelite high priest, would have to endure a rigorous cleansing process before entering. Not only would he have to fully wash himself, but he had to put on special clothing and bring burning incense, which would create smoke to block his eyes from a direct view of God. Any mishap would have resulted in severe consequences.[29]

In fact, tradition tells us that in the centuries of the temple before Jesus walked this earth, the high priest would enter the Holy of Holies with a scarlet rope tied to his foot, as well as bells around his waist. Remember, if the sins were not atoned for properly, the high priest could die in the presence of God's glory. Because no one

GOD IS INTERESTED IN THE COMPLETE REMOVAL AND DESTRUCTION OF SIN IN YOUR LIFE.

else could enter the Holy of Holies without also dying, if they needed to retrieve the body of the high priest, the rope allowed them to pull the body out. The jingle of the bells would be a sign that the priest had fallen to the ground.[30]

From the beginning of time, God has provided His people with perfect, innocent, spotless substitutes to cover up for our problems.

When Adam and Eve committed the first sin of humankind, an innocent animal shed blood and was killed to clothe them.

When Abraham's faith was being tested, and his son Isaac was about to be killed, God provided a ram in a thicket to die in Isaac's place.

When rescuing the Israelites, God instituted an annual sacrificial covenant system that required the blood of an innocent, spotless lamb.

But when the Israelites continued to fail time after time, God didn't just send another animal; He sent His one and only Son. This is why Jesus is known as the "Lamb of God." It's why John the Baptist would go around with a central message, found in John 1:29 and John 1:36: **"Look, the Lamb of God, who takes away the sin of the world!"** Jesus would live a perfect, innocent, spotless life, and by doing so would be the only perfect substitute to cover and pay for the sins of all people of all time. Including your sins.

Hebrews 9:22 tells us: **"In fact, the law requires that nearly everything be cleansed with blood, and without the shedding of blood there is no forgiveness."**

Jesus, a sinless man, substituted His life for ours, shedding His blood, and by doing so, satisfied the consequence of sin. Jesus didn't just go to the cross so you could clean cobwebs out, modify your behavior, and manage your sin. Jesus came to kill sin. A free life does not come from training your sin, but killing your sin.

In our world, we toss out the phrase "guilty by association" a lot. Sometimes, by just being in the wrong crowd or being connected to someone who fails, we get lumped in with them too. But in God's economy, through the blood of Jesus we are "innocent by association." Thanks to Jesus, your sin has been paid for, dealt with, and destroyed so you can be in the very presence of God.

When it comes to spiders and sins of all sorts, Jesus is in the extermination business.

CHALLENGE

KILL THE SPIDER

Today, identify the spider(s) that most needs to be killed in your life. Perhaps this is something you have dealt with in the past or are still dealing with now. After naming your spider, identify what the cobwebs are around it and how this spider creeps into your life.

Pray this prayer:

> *"God, I ask you to kill the spider named _____* in my life. Thank you for imparting to me the same Holy Spirit power that brought Jesus from the grave. This assures me that even though sin and temptation will be all around me, you have given me everything I need to continually kill this spider in my life."*

*This should not be the name of a person. If you are tempted to put a person's name here, ask yourself, "What is it about this person, or relationship, that needs to be dealt with?" Oftentimes, the people in our lives who are bad for us spiritually are the cobwebs, not the spiders.

11/40

DAY 12

The answer to every spiritual problem that exists in this world is always found in Jesus.

Sin is the problem. Jesus is the answer. Today, we explore how the love and grace of Jesus offers us a second chance, something that every one of us needs.

Let's jump back into the story of Peter. After Peter had failed Jesus so badly, especially with how much Jesus entrusted, empowered, and believed in him, you would think that would be the end of his story. You might think this because, in our world, sadly, many stories are ended by sin.

Not only does sin come in and take root in our lives, but labels get cast on you that identify you by your sin. The world wants to tell you that you can never bounce back from that sin, whatever that sin is for you.

Peter should have forever gone down as the denier.

As we look to Peter's blunders, we have spent considerable time this week looking to our own failures. Perhaps your failures are public for others to see, and perhaps you are even labeled, or known, for your sin. Maybe your worst failures are private, so the one slapping labels on you isn't someone else. It's you. What labels are you carrying? If sin were to end your story, how would you be remembered? As a liar? A cheat? A sleaze? An addict? An adulterer? Someone who never lived up to their potential? A waste? A bad friend? A deadbeat dad?

Everyone sins, but sin doesn't have to end your story, because God doesn't write stories that end in sin.

We can study the Bible our entire lives and never fully glean all of the amazing truths and insights contained in this living and active Word of God. There are a couple of places in the Bible, though, where what is unsaid is just as powerful as what is said.

One of those places follows John 20, the very story I introduced in *Forgiving Challenge,* in which Jesus reveals His nail-scarred hands to His disciples. After this account, it looks like John has every intention to close His Gospel. In fact, the subheading of this section reads: **The Purpose of John's Gospel.** Typically, when you are wrapping up a book, it's wise to put the main summary or purpose at the end. It makes sense to remind the readers of the "why" one last time—as we see in the next two verses that follow:

> **"Jesus performed many other signs in the presence of his disciples, which are not recorded in this book. But these are written that you may believe that Jesus is the Messiah, the Son of God, and that by believing you may have life in his name." John 20:30-31**

So Jesus came back after defeating death and sin, and He performed many more signs. What a beautiful ending to the Gospel of John. Except for one thing. It's not over. There's one more chapter. The next chapter, the final chapter of all four Gospels (Matthew, Mark, Luke and John), is the 21st chapter of John. It also happens to be the 89th chapter in all of the Gospels, and this is where we see the disciple Peter given his great, big second chance. It is in the 89th Gospel chapter where we will be spending the majority of our time over the remaining days of *Forgiving Challenge.*

But before we read it, think about the "what if" for a moment? What if there wasn't one more chapter?

If we don't have the 89th chapter, Peter would have forever gone down as the denier. His sin would be the ending of his story, and we'd be left to wonder what would have happened with the first church. Peter is the main character in the next twelve chapters of the Bible in the book of Acts. Would Jesus have chosen someone else to lead the church? And what would have been the end result of Peter's life? The truth is we don't have to ask these questions because, although it appeared to everyone that Peter's story was over, God had different plans.

When others want to label you and write your final chapter, you need to hear the truth that there's another chapter that God wants to write. Even when you listen to and are tempted to believe in the lies of the enemy—that God is finished with you—be reminded that God never writes stories with bad endings. He is the "author and finisher" of our stories. And although your story, like Peter's, may have many twists and turns, I promise you that Jesus offers you a happy ending.

God's best work comes when it appears the story is over.

J.R.R. Tolkien, the author of *The Lord of the Rings* and a devout Christian, calls the happy ending a "eucatastrophe," or a "good catastrophe." It's the joyous turn at the end of the story that gives "a fleeting glimpse of Joy, Joy beyond the walls of the world, poignant as grief."[31] Tolkien describes the birth of Christ as the eucatastrophe of human history, while the resurrection is the eucatastrophe of the incarnation. The story of Christ is the ultimate happy ending because it begins and ends in joy, he says. God wants the same for us—a joyous beginning with our birth and joyous ending with our resurrection.

There have been 88 beautiful chapters of Gospel, but it's in the 89th chapter, the last chapter, that gives us the most beautiful, relational story of forgiveness of Jesus that we have. It is the "joyous turn" that Tolkien talks about.

In the 88th chapter, Peter was in the room with Jesus where the Lord displayed his nail-scarred hands to all of the disciples. But it took the 89th chapter of the Gospels for Peter to deal with the sins that wounded him. Thank God that when everyone else wants to declare that our story is over, God simply writes another chapter.

Your challenge, which you will jump into shortly, will be to read the entire 89th chapter. It's imperative that you spend your time reading through this chapter because this story will be our anchor text for the remainder of these 40 days.

This amazing chapter starts with these four beautiful words of grace:

"Afterward Jesus appeared again..." John 21:1a

When it appears your story is over, Jesus appears again to write a new chapter.

The mere fact that Jesus appears after sin, the fact that He shows up after our failures, gives us the very hope that we cling to in our stories. Our freedom experience does not take place because of our willpower and desire, but solely because we have a God who is willing to appear again to us.

Even after they buried Jesus dead in a tomb, He still found a way to appear. His appearance wasn't smoke and mirrors. It was God in the flesh—dead but alive again. Nothing, not even death, can stop Jesus from appearing again. And again. And again.

As the Psalmist sang in Psalm 139:8 (NLT): **"If I go up to the heavens, you are there; if I make my bed in the depths, you are there."** God shows up wherever we are. Mountaintop or valley low, Jesus is there.

Our sin separates us from God. But this 40-day challenge is about bringing you back into right relationship with God, which will ultimately bring you freedom to live in this world. The path to freedom is not something you can initiate, however. It's something that God has to initiate. And the Good News: He already has. Jesus has already taken the first step toward you.

No matter how far you are down the path of sin, Jesus will not leave you. He will show up, and He will offer His grace to you. Again and again and again.

CHALLENGE

READ CHAPTER 89

The 89th chapter will serve as an integral part of our journey to freedom through God's forgiveness. The challenge today is to read the 89th chapter (John 21) and answer the following questions. We have printed the entire chapter for you on pages 270-271.

What is the main point of this story?

_____

What are three things that stuck out to you from the first reading of the 89th chapter?

1 _____

2 _____

3 _____

What does this chapter mean for Peter?

_____

What does this chapter mean for you?

_____

Because of how powerful this chapter will be in the course of our 40-day challenge, I encourage you to write down the words of the 89th chapter. You can also find a free PDF printout of the 89th chapter on our website: **www.forgivingchallenge.com/resources**. After you are done, share it on social media using #ForgivingChallenge and #Chapter89.

12/40

DAYS
13-19
OF THE 40-DAY

CHALLENGE

S.C.A.R.S.

CONFE

SSION

DAY 13

CONFESSION ALTERNATIVES

Scientists discovered that animals have two different reactions when they feel threatened or are in dangerous situations. They will respond with a "fight or flight" mentality. They will either attack or flee. God has even designed some animals' bodies to look their scariest when they are planning to fight:

- The hippo will open its mouth to reveal its massive teeth.

- The lizard will puff up its neck.

- The rattlesnake will rattle its tail.

Other animals display a "flight" reaction through unique behaviors:

- The possum will play dead.

- The chameleon will change colors, attempting to disappear.

Humans may have similar reactions when we experience conflict. Some of you may clench your fists, grit it out, or think of how to get even. This is a fight reaction. Others want to flee the situation by ignoring the pain, pretending it didn't happen.

The flight reaction is perfectly encapsulated in a cruel practical joke that Sir Arthur Conan Doyle (author of Sherlock Holmes) played on friends—although it is probably an urban legend. He sent a telegram to twelve friends with the words,

"We are discovered. Flee!" Supposedly, after receiving this telegram, all twelve friends fled and ran far away.[32] The point of this urban legend is to remind us that we all have sin in our life. These twelve friends had all done something wrong, and rather than facing the consequences, they chose to flee.

When it comes to our sin, just like with conflict, these are the two ways we naturally want to respond. Many will try to fight against it with everything they have, and others will try to run as far away from it as they can.

However, you do not help your progress along the path to God's freedom by using your own strength to fight sin or by running as far away from your mistakes as you can.

Every one of us sins. It's what we do after our sin that makes all the difference.

Many don't experience the freedom that God has for them because they don't take the necessary next step of confession. Before we dive deep into why confession is important, let's first explore four alternatives to confession that people often choose. All four of these responses fall into a "fight or flight" response, and all four are empty wells that will leave us thirsty and unsatisfied.

FIGHT: BLAMING OTHERS

We can go all the way back to the very first sin of humankind, committed by Adam and Eve, to see why we are so prone to blaming others. Although they were given an entire garden of trees and fruit to eat from, they chose to eat fruit from the one tree that God commanded them to avoid. After committing this clear act of rebellion, instead of taking responsibility for their sin, they blamed each other. When confronted with their sin, Adam actually takes a shot at not only his wife, Eve, but even at God.

"The man said, 'The woman you put here with me—she gave me some fruit from the tree, and I ate it.'" Genesis 3:12

You gave me the woman, he said, as if blaming God. And the woman gave me the fruit. Not my fault. Eve follows suit by blaming the devil.

"The woman said, 'The serpent deceived me, and I ate.'" Genesis 3:13b

Do you ever wonder why we so often say, "The devil made me do it"? Eve taught us this trick.

Other people and circumstances in our lives certainly influence the decisions we make, but it is a very dangerous practice and slippery slope that we walk on when we refuse to take responsibility for our own actions.

FIGHT: TRYING HARDER

"I just can't forgive myself…God could never forgive someone like me." Have you ever said this? Or thought this? Believe it or not, while it may appear noble on the outside, this is a form of reverse pride that is extremely dangerous. What you are proclaiming with a thought like this is that you are in a special category of people, or your sins are in a special category of sins that God cannot ultimately conquer. This thought displays a lack of faith by declaring that as big as God's grace is, it's not big enough for you.

When you pursue this line of thinking, it's natural to believe that if God cannot save you, then you will have to try to save yourself by your own self-righteous efforts. You make your life all about adhering to the Law of God and racking up as many good works as possible. Sadly, a lot of self-confessed sinners go down this empty, exhausting path. A LifeWay research study asked self-confessed sinners what they are doing about their sin. They found that only 37 percent of Christians marked "depending on Jesus Christ to overcome sin," while 38 percent of Christians marked "working on being less of a sinner."[33]

This approach will only imprison you further, because it is impossible to save yourself. Don't hear me wrong: It's a noble pursuit to live a life of good works and adhere to God's Law, but we should do these works out of compulsion by how good our God has been to us—not to earn our salvation. The only thing that trying harder to save yourself will do is leave you exhausted.

The Gospel is not about trying harder; it's about trusting.

FLIGHT: DENYING YOUR SIN

The ultimate "flight" response to sin is to flat-out deny it. If Satan can convince us that we have not sinned, then there is nothing inside of us that compels us to confess or change anything in our lives. When we deny that we are sinful, we miss out on experiencing the total freedom and healing that Jesus offers to us. According to a recent Lifeway research study, "2 out of 3 Americans confess to being a sinner (67%). The rest don't see themselves as sinners (8%), don't think sin exists (10%), or preferred not to answer the question (15%)."[34]

Satan is known as the "father of lies," and he has been working overtime the past few decades teaching moral relativism and rejecting universal truth. It's getting easier and easier to find people who will whole-heartedly accept you for who you are and even embrace the sinful parts of you that should not be embraced or encouraged. Even more depressing is that there are many Christians, and even churches, that have bought into the lies and are now spreading them.

While this 40-day challenge will ultimately help you experience freedom and even challenge you to use the freedom from your sins to bring glory to God, nowhere in this book will you find me celebrating you for your sin or helping you believe that you are not sinful.

FLIGHT: MINIMIZING YOUR SIN

It's easy to come up with excuses and find ways to justify why we committed a sin in the first place. To make ourselves feel better, rather than working our way through the freedom process, many of us try to take a shortcut by simply believing our sin was not a big deal. How many of these excuses have you used?

"I WAS YOUNG AND WILD."

"I HAD NO CHOICE."

"IT WAS JUST ONE NIGHT OF LOVE."

"IT WAS JUST ONE WEBSITE."

"EVERYONE ELSE WAS DOING IT."

"I JUST WANTED TO TRY IT ONCE."

In all of these statements, we are trying to minimize the seriousness of our sin. By minimizing our sin, not only do we minimize the sacrifice of God's Son Jesus, but we also make ourselves more susceptible to the enemy's attacks. Remember, what many people may deem to be a small sin, is still a sin.

Robert Murray M'Cheyne, an old Scottish preacher, once wrote, "I must never think a sin too small to need immediate application to the blood of Christ."[35]

Some of the worst sin habits and addictions often start with something that feels small and innocent. Sin, unless properly dealt with, always escalates.

THE ONLY THING
THAT TRYING
HARDER TO SAVE
YOURSELF WILL
DO IS LEAVE YOU
EXHAUSTED.

#FORGIVINGCHALLENGE

The devil wants you to take your guilt and bring more shame into your lives. Any pursuit of blaming others, trying harder, denying your sin, or minimizing your sin will ultimately keep you in bondage. Here's why: You are guilty.

The beautiful truth about God and His Gospel is that you don't have to run from your sin any longer. God wants you to face it, but He doesn't need you to fight it. He's already won the battle for you by fighting and destroying sin.

You were saved by grace alone through faith alone. Matt Chandler writes, "Therefore, God gets all the glory alone. And when you understand this one basic issue, you'll stop going into you and start going into the Lord—just laying out all the smelly, rotten groceries, shaking all the stuff out of your pockets, bringing it all out into the open, and saying, 'Here, would you please get rid of this for me?' If your spouse or your kids or your boss or your parents ever pick out a piece of your character or attitude that needs fixing, you can just take your pitiful self straight before Him and say, 'Jesus, come and get it.' Because your satisfaction comes from His work, not yours."[36]

Your sin will imprison you. but the grace of Jesus will free you.

CHALLENGE

WHAT'S YOUR ALTERNATIVE?

1 Are you more prone to a fight or flight mentality when it comes to conflict? Why?

_____

_____

_____

2 Which of the four confession alternatives are you most likely to use: Blame, Try Harder, Deny, or Minimize?

_____

_____

_____

3 How have any of these alternatives worked out for you in the past?

_____

_____

_____

4 Memorize Romans 6:23: **"For the wages of sin is death, but the gift of God is eternal life in Christ Jesus our Lord."**

13/40

DAY 14

SPOILER ALERT

I'm going to tell you the ending of the movie *Lion King*.

Before you give a spoiler to a movie, there is an unwritten rule that you must allow two to four weeks after the movie is released. Well, this one's been out for well over 1,000 weeks, so you've had your chance to see either the original animated version, the stage version, or the live-action remake!

There is a moment in *Lion King* where the main character, Simba, as a young lion, watched his dad, Mufasa, die. Even though he was not the main culprit in his father's death, his willful defiance did contribute to the chaos of this moment. So he blamed himself. And what did he do in response to this? He ran.

In self-inflicted exile, Simba lived a different life, but it wasn't the worst life ever. He wasn't a horrible guy. Simba didn't live a life of crime, drugs, and passion. He made friends with a warthog named Pumbaa and a meercat known as Timon. Hakuna Matata. But he was miles from where he should have been. What's more, he spent years surrounding himself with distractions and entertainment to try to wall out his shame, and he abandoned a world that desperately needed him to engage.[37]

Why do I share that with you?

I've been in ministry long enough to know that this is the all-too-common response for many people who have followed Jesus at one point in their lives. There was something, some moment, when things changed for them. They used to follow Jesus and may have been involved in ministry. They might have served on mission trips, participated in the youth group, or even felt a call of God on their lives. But something happened, and they simply stopped pursuing Jesus with the same passion.

Typically, that "some moment" or that "something" or that "some date" when everything changed was a sin. For some, it was their own personal sin—a sin that made them feel disqualified and unworthy to live up to the calling Jesus placed in their life. So what did they do? They just walked away from their calling. They didn't become the worst person ever. They're actually still contributing to society. They've still got some things going for them. But they've gone down a different path.

This is my story as well. I've done the same thing. I've been close with God, received His forgiveness, and understood the call of God on my life. But because of my own sin, I simply didn't see myself worthy. I faded away and started going a different direction. I was still a "good guy," making a good contribution to society. I was just going down a different path. My wake-up call was the car accident that I wrote about in the introduction, which ended with a scar underneath my chin.

If this story feels all too real for you, may today be God's wake-up call.

Let's enter back into our anchor text for the series in John 21…

"Afterward Jesus appeared again to his disciples, by the Sea of Galilee. It happened this way: Simon Peter, Thomas (also known as Didymus), Nathanael from Cana in Galilee, the sons of Zebedee, and two other disciples were together. 'I'm going out to fish,' Simon Peter told them, and they said, 'We'll go with you.'" John 21:1-3

After his denials of Jesus prior to the crucifixion, Peter goes back to fishing. Having failed, Peter goes back to a mediocre, lesser life than God had called him to. There is nothing wrong with fishing for fish, except if God has called you to fish for something greater. After we've failed, too many of us believe in the lie of the enemy that says we are unfit and unworthy of what God had originally called us into, so we go back to a lesser life.

Scholars debate the significance of Peter going back to fishing and what it means. I resonate with Pastor Ben Stuart's insight. He says, "Some think he's just passing time. That this isn't a big deal. Now, if he's just throwing a line in and hoping to get a bite, that's one thing. But it says that they were fishing all night. You also have to look at the greater context of who this is and what he is saying. This is Peter saying 'I am fishing.'"[38]

If I walked into my living room tomorrow and said to my wife, Allison, "I'm going to play basketball," she would assume that I would go to the local gym and shoot around or try to get into a pickup game. In either case, I would do my absolute best as a 6-foot 1-inch, 38-year-old man with a sore back, to get the ball into the hoop. And she would be right. Nowhere in my statement, "I'm going to play basketball," would she think, "Oh Zach's entering the NBA draft." She knows me, and context matters.

I'm old enough to remember Michael Jordan, the second greatest basketball player of all-time (behind LeBron James). After his unfortunate little foray into baseball, Jordan said the exact same sentence that I used: "I'm going to play basketball." No one in that room said, "Wait, like at the local gym? With your kids? Are you playing HORSE?" Everyone knew that MJ meant he's back running with the Bulls from Chicago again.

Peter was a lifetime fisherman. Fishing was all that he knew. Even though Jesus invited him into another life, Peter failed Jesus badly. And in light of that, he said, "I'm going fishing." He just dove back into something that he felt like he could win at. That's what we often do when we fail. Unless we experience God's freedom, most of us, after sin, will just pinball from distractions and busyness and step away from what God wants to do in our lives. We move into what is comfortable—a slow bleed into a lesser, mediocre life than what God had intended.

The other sad piece about Peter's decision is that he rallied other disciples to go back to fishing with him. Peter's still a leader. When we fail, when we fall back, we tend to drag others back down with us. Many of us think our sin just affects us. No, it doesn't. You influence others, just as others influence you.

Hurt people tend to hurt people.

"So they went out and got into the boat, but that night they caught nothing." John 21:3b

Failing to catch fish is not a coincidence. Think about this: On the boat were six men with a history of fishing. They didn't catch a single fish the entire night on a sea that they knew like the back of their hands. They must've felt embarrassed. But sometimes the things we think are a disgrace are actually beautiful displays of God's grace.

God's grace works in unusual ways. Sometimes God starts the path of freedom by complicating things. If you are on a path that leads to destruction, whether that's a slow bleed or a freight train moving fast, God will usually begin by complicating things in His pursuit of you.

"Early in the morning, Jesus stood on the shore, but the disciples did not realize that it was Jesus. He called out to them, 'Friends, haven't you any fish?'" John 21:4-5a

On this day, fishing is not really working for them, is it?

"'No,' they answered." John 21:5b

I also don't think they're in the mood for a long conversation at this point. A one-word answer. "No."

"He said, 'Throw your net on the right side of the boat and you will find some.'" John 21:6a

At this point, the disciples didn't know this was Jesus speaking, so I can imagine what they must've been thinking: "Ya, sure, okay man...why don't you stick to whatever you got cooking over there! We know how to fish." And yet, for some strange reason, they listened to Jesus's advice, still not knowing it was Him, and look at what happened:

"When they did, they were unable to haul the net in because of the large number of fish." John 21:6b

In the aftermath of Peter's greatest failure, what does Jesus do? He appears to him on the shore, and He recreates the very first moment that He met Peter. When Jesus meets Peter in Luke 5:1-11, He tells him to go out into deep water and let down his nets, even though the disciples had worked all night without catching anything. When they obey, they catch so many fish that their nets begin to break. Sound familiar? (We'll look at this first encounter in the Challenge that follows.) In John 21, Jesus recreates the same fish miracle to remind Peter that their relationship is still open, and the opportunity is still there for him.

It's the same with you…how does Jesus treat you in your failure? He appears to you and reminds you that the opportunity is still there for you.

Why would you let sin spoil you when Jesus offers to divide the spoils of fish with you today?

CHALLENGE

THE FIRST FISH MIRACLE

Go back and read the first time that Jesus met Peter—Luke 5:1-11:

"One day as Jesus was standing by the Lake of Gennesaret [Sea of Galilee], the people were crowding around him and listening to the word of God. He saw at the water's edge two boats, left there by the fishermen, who were washing their nets. He got into one of the boats, the one belonging to Simon, and asked him to put out a little from shore. Then he sat down and taught the people from the boat.

"When he had finished speaking, he said to Simon, 'Put out into deep water, and let down the nets for a catch.'

"Simon answered, 'Master, we've worked hard all night and haven't caught anything. But because you say so, I will let down the nets.'

"When they had done so, they caught such a large number of fish that their nets began to break. So they signaled their partners in the other boat to come and help them, and they came and filled both boats so full that they began to sink.

"When Simon Peter saw this, he fell at Jesus' knees and said, 'Go away from me, Lord; I am a sinful man!' For he and all his companions were astonished at the catch of fish they had taken, and so were James and John, the sons of Zebedee, Simon's partners.

"Then Jesus said to Simon, 'Don't be afraid; from now on you will fish for people.' So they pulled their boats up on shore, left everything and followed him."

1 How is this story similar to **#Chapter89** (John 21)?

_____

_____

_____

2 How is this story different from **#Chapter89** (John 21)?

_____

_____

_____

3 When you have failed in the past, do you tend to rise back to the occasion or retreat to where you were?

_____

_____

_____

4 Looking back over your story, has there ever been a time where God worked mysteriously by complicating things in your life? Explain.

_____

_____

_____

14/40

DAY 15

'FESS UP TO THE MESS-UP

One of the most impactful pieces of evidence in a criminal case is the suspect's confession. If you can get the suspect to confess to a crime, it will have an extraordinary effect on the jury's final verdict. Because of this, if you've watched any Netflix crime documentary, you will know the lengths that some authorities will go to in order to capture a confession. Experiments have shown that even if a confession is coerced, it will almost always sway the jury against the accused.

Confessions in the modern-day courtroom lead to prison sentences.

Therefore, you may feel like the worst step you could take in your journey to find freedom would be to confess your sins. But God's justice system doesn't work the same as our justice system today.

In God's justice system, confession of sin will not lead to a prison sentence, but to a life of freedom.

Freedom begins with an admission of sin.

King David is one of the most prominent characters in all of the Bible. He is described in 1 Samuel 13:14 as a "man after God's own heart," which is a shocking statement because David had a long list of egregious sins. After committing an act of adultery, rather than confessing this sin and facing the consequences, he piled on sin after sin to try to cover it up. Every sin led to further bondage. His sin of adultery led to deception, lies, and debauchery. When these sins didn't get rid of his problem, he actually set up the murder of the man whose wife he slept with. This is a man after God's own heart?

David did so many things wrong, but one thing David did right is admitting to just how wrong he had been. Tired of living a double life, he returned to God, who was always there for Him. His words from Psalm 32:3-5 (NLT) are a beautiful picture of our lives before and after we confess our sins.

> **"When I refused to confess my sin,**
> **my body wasted away,**
> **and I groaned all day long.**
> **Day and night your hand of discipline was heavy on me.**
> **My strength evaporated like water in the summer heat.**
>
> **"Finally, I confessed all my sins to you**
> **and stopped trying to hide my guilt.**
> **I said to myself, 'I will confess my rebellion to the Lord.'**
> **And you forgave me! All my guilt is gone."**

In those three verses, you can see what life is like Before Confession (BC) of sins and After Declaration (AD) of sins:

A BC PERSON:

- Body wasting away
- Continual groaning
- Constant heaviness upon him
- Strength evaporating
- Hiding guilt

AN AD PERSON:

- Fully forgiven
- Guilt-free

As you study these two persons, which one looks free to you? Which one do you feel more like today?

Just as our calendar was forever changed upon Christ's entrance into this world, we too are forever changed when we allow Christ to work His declaration of forgiveness over our words of confession. We become a new man or a new woman after God's own heart.

The Bible is filled with flawed characters who can't seem to get out of their own way. Through characters with checkered pasts like David, Abraham, Moses, Rahab, and Paul, we learn that God not only isn't afraid of our sin, but He encourages us to bring it to Him. We learn from Peter's story that we don't have to catch God at the right time, because He's already prepared a table for us.

We have only scratched the surface of John 21 thus far, but a meal that Jesus prepared will set the stage for the eventual reinstatement of Peter. After realizing that Jesus was the man on the shore, Peter jumped out of the boat, swam to him, and found his Lord cooking fish over an open charcoal fire. (Peter had a thing about jumping out of boats, whether he was trying to walk on water or rushing to Jesus's side on the beach.)

"When they landed, they saw a fire of burning coals there with fish on it, and some bread." John 21:9

We don't know what type of fish Jesus cooked that day, nor what spices Jesus used, although tradition says it was tilapia, dubbed "St. Peter's fish." Whatever it was, I'm sure the fish tasted divine. But the significance of this meal is less about the quality of the food, and more about what would happen at this meal.

To dine with someone who caused a problem with you in ancient culture is to express forgiveness.

Not only did Jesus take the first step and appear on the shore to Peter, but He went a step further and cooked a meal for Peter. He was telling Peter with his actions, "I'm ready to forgive you. Are you ready to be forgiven?"

Jesus didn't put Peter in a dark room without windows and shine a hot lamp on him. He didn't drag him to trial and stand him in front of a judge, a jury, and the national media. What did he do? He cooked breakfast for Peter, and He invited Peter to dine with Him and taste freedom.

If you are ready to 'fess up to all of your mess-ups, Jesus has prepared a table for you. He's ready for you. The thyme is now. Stop floundering. He's got enough grouper (or tilapia) for the whole group.

CHALLENGE

MEMORIZE THE PROMISE

God promises to forgive and purify us when we confess our sins to Him. One of the clearest verses that illustrate this is words we learned first on Day 2, from 1 John 1:8-9. Today, your challenge is to commit those two verses to memory. A great way to help you memorize these verses would be to write them down and place them in a spot you frequently walk by.

"If we claim to be without sin, we deceive ourselves and the truth is not in us. If we confess our sins, he is faithful and just and will forgive us our sins and purify us from all unrighteousness."

15/40

DAY 16

CANNONBALL CONFIDENCE

My youngest son, Brady, just started playing flag football, and at the first practice, the coach named him the team's quarterback. I guess with a name like Brady, this was inevitable. Because of his new position, he constantly wants to throw the football and play catch. When Brady and I play catch, we hardly ever drop the ball. When there is no pressure, and we're just throwing the ball back and forth, it's easy to catch a ball.

A few months ago, our church youth group put together a flag football game with the students and adult leaders. I entered the game as a wide receiver, hoping to use my height advantage against many of the students who hadn't fully developed yet. I am known to do my fair share of what I like to call "wholesome smack-talking," especially when I find myself up against teenagers.

On one particular play, my quarterback threw a beautiful spiral to me that hit me in stride right in my chest. I was wide open and there was no one around me. And yet, somehow, the ball went through my hands and fell to the ground. I had dropped a surefire touchdown. At this point, I began to regret that I had been smack-talking the students, for now I was on the receiving end of their smack-talk back to me.

I still remember the feeling of dropping this pass. I felt like an idiot coming back to the huddle. The pass was perfect. How could I have dropped it?

Looking back at that moment, odds are that nobody else remembers the play. Why would they? It was a meaningless flag football scrimmage with the youth group.

This wasn't a high-stakes game. It wasn't important in the grand scheme of things. And yet, I still remember going back into the huddle feeling awful. I let my team down. If that's how we feel over something that's meaningless, how much worse do we feel when we "drop the ball" in matters that are important.

After we fail, it's easy for feelings of embarrassment and shame to come over us. It's easy for us to run further away from our problems and to lack confidence.

If you feel like you "dropped the ball" in your pursuit of following Jesus, you might feel unworthy to be in His presence. Maybe you feel a lack of confidence in approaching Jesus. But the Scriptures teach us that we don't need to come to Him with our tails between our legs; we can approach Him confidently, even after our sin.

Check out these words from Hebrews 4:16: **"Let us then approach God's throne of grace with confidence, so that we may receive mercy and find grace to help us in our time of need."**

This feels very different from what we read about on Day 11. On that day, we introduced the Old Covenant and the sacrificial system that God set up to atone for the sins of the Israelite people. Remember, the high priest, after a rigorous cleansing process, could enter the Holy of Holies only once a year to atone for the sins of all of the people. Not only this, but to further ensure distance between the holy God and an unholy people, remember that the Holy of Holies room was separated by a massive veil made of fine linen.

While we celebrate and remember many amazing things about the crucifixion and resurrection of Jesus, one often overlooked part of the story is what happens in Matthew 27:50-51a: **"And when Jesus had cried out again in a loud voice, he**

gave up his spirit. At that moment the curtain of the temple was torn in two from top to bottom."

Did you notice how the veil, or curtain, was torn at the time of His death? It was torn from top to bottom. This means the veil was not torn in half by any man. It was a supernatural miracle done by the power of God! God tore the veil from the top, so you and I could be in His presence. The reason that Jesus died on the cross was to bring you back into right relationship with God.

Josephus, a first-century Jewish historian, tells us how massive the veil was—30 feet high by 30 feet wide, as well as 4 inches thick. He says that horses tied to each side could not pull the veil apart.[39] Josephus's words are not inspired by God. He's a historian. But his writing is one more piece of evidence to show the truth of Jesus!

By tearing the curtain at the exact time in which Jesus died, God tells us, loud and clear: Through the death of Jesus on the cross, sin no longer separates us from God!

His blood now gives us access to the very presence of God.

Oftentimes we get it wrong when it comes to approaching God. We are typically taught to wear our "Sunday best" clothing to church. We are directly or indirectly taught to button-up, put on a smile, and act like everything is in order in our lives. Many churches have been created around this plastic, inauthentic, and false reality.

The more appropriate teaching is that God doesn't care how we come to Him, just that we come. Jesus's death made a way for us to approach Him. If God cared about how we came to Him, He probably would have rejected Peter.

Immediately after the miraculous catch of fish in John 21, one of the more humorous scenes in all of the Bible takes place.

"Then the disciple whom Jesus loved said to Peter, 'It is the Lord!' As soon as Simon Peter heard him say, 'It is the Lord,' he wrapped his outer garment around him (for he had taken it off) and jumped into the water." John 21:7

Six times we are introduced to "the disciple whom Jesus loved" in the Gospel of John. The "disciple whom Jesus loved" is John, so he's writing about himself here. John is the one who notices that the man on the beach is Jesus. But once Peter realizes it is Jesus, what does he do? He puts on his coat and then jumps into the water! This is not normal. You do not put on more clothing before you jump into the water, and yet this is exactly what Peter did. The Greek word for "jumping" here implies casting, throwing, or rushing. The fisherman, who is used to casting a net into the sea, now casts himself into the sea! I can imagine this wasn't a pretty dive into the water either, but more like Peter throwing himself into the water with a big splash. Cannonball!

"The other disciples followed in the boat, towing the net full of fish, for they were not far from shore, about a hundred yards." John 21:8

I can almost sense some sarcasm in John's words. He is highlighting how ridiculous Peter's jump into the water was. Their boat wasn't even that far from shore.

What can we make of this? Peter was so excited to see Jesus that he was out of his right mind. Throwing on a jacket, he hurled himself into the water and sprinted up to Jesus, soaking wet.

This is a beautiful picture to me of the proper response when we know that Jesus is available. It also shows us clearly what's going on in the heart of Peter. He's so excited it's Jesus that he will do whatever he must to get to his Lord. He doesn't need to approach Jesus fully buttoned up, with everything in order. No, he comes soaking wet to Jesus!

God is not an unapproachable God. He is a loving God who made Himself available for you by the death and resurrection of Jesus.

Rather than trying to come to God all buttoned up, as if everything is perfect, what if you just came to God however you are today?

Mike Foster writes, "God doesn't ask us to first clean up our sloppy messes. He does not approach us with a guarded politeness or condescendingly pat us on the head and squeeze our dirty cheeks. He simply invites us to jump into Daddy's arms and let Him be our source of love and identity. He beckons us to live the free way."[40]

Just like Peter, He'll take you as you are, but His grace will not leave you as you are.

CHALLENGE

BE CONFIDENT

Now that we have a greater understanding of atonement through the Old and New Covenants, read through Hebrews 10 and answer the following questions:

1 How do you typically see God?

☐ ANGRY   ☐ KIND

☐ UNAPPROACHABLE   ☐ NEAR

☐ DISTANT   ☐ _____

☐ LOVING   ☐ _____

2 How do you normally approach God?

☐ CONFIDENT   ☐ MESSY

☐ FEARFUL   ☐ CLEAN

3 Is there anything keeping you from approaching God today?

_____

_____

_____

_____

_____

16/40

DAY 17

CONFESSION THROUGH CONCESSION

Thus far, we've seen the sin of Peter in full display. Now it's time for Peter to confess his sins to Jesus to receive forgiveness.

However, there is one problem. If you go back and peruse the story in John 21, nowhere in this account do we see an apology or words that would typically come with a confession.

We are taught that when you do wrong, you need to say the words, "I'm sorry," followed by the words, "Will you forgive me?" As parents, we teach our children the importance of saying these words. We then watch them trudge over to their brother or sister and begrudgingly, under their breath with a frown on their face, mumble the words, "I'm sorry."

One tradition my wife and I have added is that after the words are exchanged, we tell our two boys to hug. They hate doing this, and yet something about their hatred of this idea makes me love it all the more. I told you, I'm a sinner like you! Nevertheless, I believe it's wise and appropriate parenting to ask our children to go through this exercise. But do you think our kids actually mean the words that they are saying? If your kids are anything like mine, not usually. They are simply going through the motions to satisfy the requirements that their mom and dad have placed on them.

In many churches, including the tradition I've grown up in, the service each week begins with reading the same words of confession. I have to admit that, although there are times I have read those words aloud and meant every word, there are other times when I'm simply going through the motions.

I bring this up because we would expect to hear from Peter the words, "I'm sorry, Jesus, please forgive me." But nowhere do we hear them.

What can we learn from this? Was Peter really sorry?

On the night that Peter denied Jesus, after the third and final denial followed by the rooster crowing (just as Jesus predicted), Luke records these words:

> **"At that moment the Lord turned and looked at Peter. Suddenly, the Lord's words flashed through Peter's mind: 'Before the rooster crows tomorrow morning, you will deny three times that you even know me.' And Peter left the courtyard, weeping bitterly." Luke 22:61-62 (NLT)**

The words "weeping bitterly" in Greek could also mean "wailing aloud violently." Peter knew he failed Jesus and was deeply sorrowful. I'm sure that in the aftermath of the crucifixion of Jesus, all the way up to the 89th chapter of the Gospels, Peter had replayed that scenario over and over and over again. Typically, when we fail badly, we replay these moments in our minds endlessly.

Another place we see the sorrow of Peter is in the exchange that takes place by the charcoal fire on the beach. Look at what John 21:17 says:

> **"A third time he [Jesus] asked him, 'Simon son of John, do you love me?' "Peter was hurt that Jesus asked the question a third time. He said, 'Lord, you know everything. You know that I love you.'" (NLT)**

Looking into the Greek text, we find that the word "hurt" could also mean "pain, grieve, or deeply hurt." Sorrow is there. But still, we don't have the exact words, "I'm sorry." We don't have the confession. Is there something more at play here?

Looking at the context and character of Peter reveals an important truth not widely taught when it comes to confessing our sins to God. Peter is a man known for his confessions. I would argue that up to this point Peter has had the single best confession and the single worst confession in all of the Gospels.

The best confession? We read about this on Day 7. This was in Matthew 16:13-19, where Jesus asked Peter, **"Who do you say I am?"** Peter replied, **"You are the Messiah, the Son of Living God."** Jesus was so pleased with this declarative statement that he said back to Peter, **"On this rock I will build my church, and the gates of Hades will not overcome it."** This was the confession on which Jesus built His church. The greatest confession in the Gospels.

The worst confession was the first time Jesus performed the fish miracle. The disciples were out fishing all night, and they caught nothing. Jesus mysteriously shows up, tells them to cast their nets on the other side, and they have a miraculous catch of fish. When this happened, look at what Peter confessed.

> **"When Simon Peter saw this, he fell at Jesus' knees and said, 'Go away from me, Lord; I am a sinful man!'" Luke 5:8**

This is a terrible confession. To his credit, Peter got it half right: "I'm a sinful man." But then he asked Jesus to go away from him. That's the worst possible outcome you could ask for in a confession to God. The very thing he asks Jesus to do is the very thing that would have ultimately led to his destruction.

Amazingly, despite this awful confession, Jesus responded to Peter with an invitation to follow Him and come near to Him. Peter asked Jesus to go away, and then Jesus gave him an opportunity to come near. He tells Peter that from now on he will be a fisher of men.

What do we see in these two stories and also scattered throughout the Gospels? Peter was never afraid to speak. He was not one to mince words, even if he didn't completely think through the words coming out of his mouth. Sometimes he got his words SO right, and sometimes he got his words SO wrong. You could say that Peter had the spiritual gift of opening his mouth!

However, when the conversation by the charcoal fire in John 21 begins, Jesus takes the initiative and only then does Peter respond. Peter doesn't speak first and think later. None of that. But note that Peter also doesn't say the words, "I'm sorry." While we don't have the precise words of an actual confession, we finally have Peter's concession. He doesn't try to come up with excuses. He simply professes his love for Jesus, and this speaks volumes about what was going on in his heart.

God knows your heart. There is no fooling Him. He's ready to hear your confession should you have the words to express it. But even when you don't have the words to express your sorrow and regret, God can look even deeper into your heart. There are no magic words to say. Your heart says it all.

Rather than coming to God with a perfectly scripted confession, what if you just came to God with your heart right now? God can handle flawed confessions. What's most important is that you simply come back to Him. Even when you have nothing to say, He will fill you with His grace.

CONFESSION TIME!

Sometimes, when we don't have the words to speak our confession, it's important to look at the words of someone who has gone before us. Below is an example of a confession I have said in many worship services in the past. Sometimes I have said these words with good motives and other times as ritual. I have found, however, that when I slow down with these words, they tend to be more powerful.

Today, read through this confession one sentence at a time and pause. Pray after each line. Without feeling the need to script anything beautifully, record your thoughts, feelings, or emotions after each line.

Most merciful God, we confess that we are by nature sinful and unclean.

_____

_____

We have sinned against You in thought, word, and deed, by what we have done and by what we have left undone.

_____

_____

We have not loved You with our whole heart; we have not loved our neighbors as ourselves.

_____

_____

We justly deserve Your present and eternal punishment.

_____

_____

For the sake of Your Son, Jesus Christ, have mercy on us.

_____

_____

Forgive us, renew us, and lead us, so that we may delight in Your will and walk in Your ways to the glory of Your holy name. Amen.[41]

_____

_____

Next, hear this declaration from God to you, based on His promise in 1 John 1:8-9, which you memorized on Day 15:

> *"Almighty God in His mercy has given His Son to die for you and for His sake forgives you all your sins. You have been forgiven in the name of the Father, by the blood of the Son, and through the power of the Holy Spirit. Amen."*

17/40

DAY 18

CONFESSION HELPS YOUR CONFESSION

Did you know that the word "confession" has more than one meaning?

To confess means:

1 TO ADMIT OR STATE THAT ONE HAS COMMITTED A CRIME OR IS AT FAULT IN SOME WAY.

2 TO DECLARE ONE'S RELIGIOUS FAITH.[42]

We've primarily been discussing the first type of confession this week. Today, I want to talk about how these two types of confession can work together. I want to show how one type of confession can help the other form of confession.

In the Christian church, we collectively have "confessions of faith" that we proclaim together. These are known as creeds. The typical creeds of the church are the Apostles Creed, the Nicene Creed, and the lesser-known Athanasian creed. The word "creed" comes from the Latin word "credo" meaning "I believe," and these creeds are meant to be a concise summary of our faith.

While creeds serve an important role for the collective church to speak together, it's also important that each of us, as individuals, understand how to confess our faith and share our story. God has been so great to us that each of us have a unique story, or testimony, to share with others.

Our ultimate end goal in this world is that we would continue to become greater followers of Jesus. As we take steps toward being and behaving more like Jesus, He will be more greatly glorified in our lives. The five targets that followers of Jesus should ascribe to, as taught in *Red Letter Challenge*, are "Being, Forgiving, Serving, Giving, and Going."

"Going" implies that we are called to not just physically go, but also to speak and share the Good News of Jesus with others. Near the end of all four Gospels, Jesus gives a "going" charge to the disciples.

> **Matthew 28:19a:** "Go and make disciples..."
> **Mark 16:15:** "Go into all the world and preach the gospel to all creation."
> **Luke 24:48:** "You are witnesses of these things..."
> **John 20:21b:** "As the Father has sent me, I am sending you."

There are only a few words of Jesus in the book of Acts. His final words come right before He ascends, when Jesus speaks to His disciples in Acts 1:8:

> **"But you will receive power when the Holy Spirit comes on you; and you will be my witnesses in Jerusalem, and in all Judea and Samaria, and to the ends of the earth."**

The final thing that Jesus tells His disciples is that they are called to be His witnesses. What is a witness? Someone who speaks and testifies to what they have seen.

At the root of what Jesus asks His followers is that we who have received the Good News of Jesus should go and share it with others. And yet, from our research of thousands of people who have completed our FREE *Red Letter Challenge Assessment* (**www.redletterchallenge.com/rlc-assessment**), the data inform us that out of all five targets we ascribe to excel in, collectively we are the worst at "going." So how in the world can confessing our sins help us with this?

Amazingly, a Christian research company found that those who were most likely to spread the Good News had a regular practice of confession in their lives. Those most willing to talk about and spread the Good News of Jesus started with an understanding that they are the ones most in need of God's grace.[43]

When you confess your sins to God, it makes you stronger in confessing your faith to others.

Why is this?

Along with a regular practice of confession comes a regular reminder of not only our brokenness, but God's kindness. Paul tells us in Romans 2:4 (MSG): **"God is kind, but he's not soft. In kindness he takes us firmly by the hand and leads us into a radical life-change."**

When you cry out to God, you are confessing that not only are you in need, but you believe God has what you need. Sometimes in our confession, it's what we don't say that says just as much.

When we regularly experience the kindness and grace of God in our lives, it keeps us in a place where we remain grateful for the gift God gives to us. The longer some of us have been in Christ, typically, the harder it is to keep the childlike faith and wonder that we had when we first received the grace of God. A regular practice of confession is a helpful and necessary reminder of just how amazing the grace of Jesus is in our lives.

By regularly confessing your brokenness and receiving God's kindness in your story, you will become more effective at the confession of faith you give to the world. Also, this practice will keep you ready and able to confess your faith to others.

This is, after all, not only what Jesus charged us with, but it's also what our guy, Peter, would sum up beautifully in 1 Peter 3:15:

"Always be prepared to give an answer to everyone who asks you to give the reason for the hope that you have."

Are you prepared to do this? Are you ready to give this answer? If not, perhaps your answer could materialize by practicing daily confession to God every day.

Do you know how to confess your sins? Yesterday, we taught that it's less about how you come to God, but that you simply come to Him. While at times we may not have the words, or we borrow the confessions of others who have gone before us, I believe it is important to understand what a confession, or an apology, looks like. God can see into our hearts, but not all people can. Therefore, an appropriate confession typically includes all three of these steps:

1. ADMIT YOUR FAULT.

Own what you did. Don't make excuses. Don't blame it on someone else. Don't say, "I did this because you did _____." Simply own your part.

2. SHOW YOUR SORROW.

With words, expressions, and body language, declare why you are filled with sorrow. Help the other person know that you now understand the hurt caused by your actions or inactions. This also indicates a willingness for repentance—admitting a desire to change in the future.

3. ASK FOR FORGIVENESS.

Don't assume it will be given. Give the offended the opportunity, or choice, to declare words of forgiveness over you. Ask, "Will you forgive me?"

When we confess to God, He will always forgive. And as we grow in receiving His grace for ourselves, we too will become more forgiving people.

CHALLENGE

CONFESS YOUR FAITH

What sins are you having a hard time moving past?

Confess them now before God using these three steps as a guide. You can choose to write your confession below or speak it out loud to God.

1 ADMIT YOUR FAULT.

2 SHOW YOUR SORROW.

3 ASK FOR FORGIVENESS.

_____

_____

_____

_____

_____

_____

_____

When finished, read the words of the Apostle's Creed. (This can easily be found by using an online search engine.)

18/40

DAY 19

BE WEAK EVERY WEEK

Can I make a confession? I probably should have said this on the first day of this week's readings, but confession is hard. Personally, I've never found it easy or fun to admit that I have done something wrong. Oftentimes, freedom in Jesus comes not by doing what's easy or fun, but what's necessary.

At any point at any time, we can go directly to God to confess. We can approach Him confidently. In confession, we also have the promise that He will listen, and He will respond in kindness by giving us His grace. We ought to go to Him on a daily basis.

Throughout the New Testament, however, God also encourages us to go to one another to confess our sins. Nowhere is this clearer than in the words of Jesus's brother, in James 5:16:

> **"Therefore confess your sins to each other and pray for each other so that you may be healed. The prayer of a righteous person is powerful and effective."**

This amazing principle is found all throughout the Bible: God doesn't need us to ultimately fulfill His mission, but He invites us to be a part of it. When it comes to confession, God is the one who works the miracle, but He invites you and me into this process. It may be difficult to confess your sins to God, but I have found it far more difficult to confess my sins to another human being. It is humbling and scary, but it's an important part of the ultimate healing process.

Part of being set free is confessing to one other person. As Rick Warren says, "Revealing your feeling is the beginning of healing."[44]

We live in a nation that celebrates strength, so admitting weakness is perceived as exactly that—weak. But truthfully, when we admit we are weak, God is most powerful. Our weaknesses only give God a greater chance to shine, and our ultimate goal and pursuit in this life is to glorify God. Nothing gives God the opportunity to receive more glory than allowing His light to shine in our darkest places.

The apostle Paul said it this way in 2 Corinthians 12:9: **"My grace is sufficient for you, for my power is made perfect in weakness. Therefore, I will boast all the more gladly about my weaknesses, so that Christ's power may rest on me."**

When we present our weaknesses to God, we give Him an opportunity to move mightily in our lives. May we never forget that it's God who will ultimately provide the miracle of forgiveness in our lives. And yet, even with this knowledge, Jesus still invites each of His disciples to be an integral part of the process.

Mike Foster, in his book *Freeway*, says, "As we go forward, discovering the part of our hearts that hurt, we should do it with a friend. Our friends will help uncover our strengths and weaknesses. But don't let them try to fix you; just let them help get you there, because Jesus is the only fixer and freedom giver."[45]

A few years ago, after missing the mark yet again in my life, I finally did what I had been encouraging others to do for years. I asked a friend of mine if he would be willing to be my "accountability partner." As part of this, I asked him if he would faithfully check in with me weekly. I assured him that I would always be honest with him. And we resolved to ask each other these four questions:

How is your relationship and rhythms with God in the last week?

1 How is your relationship and rhythms with your family in the last week?

2 Did you look at anything you shouldn't have looked at?

3 Would your wife say anything different about the answers you just gave me?

4

I have found this practice of "being weak" every week to be extremely helpful for me on my journey of ultimately becoming a greater follower of Jesus. It doesn't mean that I don't have times in which I still miss the mark, but weekly confession helps bring healing by doing at least these four things:

1. IT DESTROYS THE ENEMY'S LIE THAT YOU ARE ALONE.

One of the strongest lies the enemy sends our way is that you are completely alone in your sin. Satan will try to make you believe that no one is missing the mark quite like you are—that if people really knew what was going on with you, they'd be shocked. The truth that I have found is that while people will often celebrate you for your strengths, they'll also resonate with you in your weaknesses. Confessing your sins to someone else brings you out of the shadows and into the light of truth. You are not alone. The more you hear the truth of the Gospel over the lies of the enemy, the better you will become as a follower.

2. IT GIVES YOU ANOTHER BOUNDARY TO CURB YOU FROM SINNING.

In our fight against sin, and ultimately to maintain freedom, it is wise to put up as many boundaries around us as possible. Part of living in the freedom of God is not only to instill the necessary habits that will ultimately put us in position to make good decisions, but also to raise the necessary boundaries around the areas in our lives where we are most prone to fall. Quite frankly, knowing that I have a weekly check-in with my accountability partner has stopped me at times from following through on a particular action that I knew would be sinful.

3. IT DESTROYS THE "HYPOCRITE" LABEL THAT OTHERS MAY WANT TO PLACE ON YOU.

Sadly, one of the labels that many Christians are known for is "hypocrites." A hypocrite is someone who says one thing but does another thing. The surefire way to avoid being a hypocrite is to confess to others that you are sinful. Admit that you are broken. People may still be able to label you a "sinner," but they cannot any further label you a hypocrite if you regularly confess your sins and talk of your shortcomings.

4. IT GIVES SOMEONE ELSE THE OPPORTUNITY TO SPEAK THE WORDS OF JESUS TO YOU.

This is a dual benefit. Not only do you, the confessor, get to hear the words of forgiveness spoken over you, but it also gives the one listening to the confession the chance to step into their calling and represent Jesus to you in this world. The more you give others a chance to step into the calling that God has for them, the more able and confident they will be in their pursuit of following Jesus.

Do you have someone in your life with whom you can be real? That you can confess your sins to? We can go to Jesus at any time, but Jesus also gives us the Body of Christ, filled with brothers and sisters, who can help us on our journey of receiving freedom. I love what Matt Chandler says: "To be 99% known is to not be fully known."[46] Aren't you ready to be fully known?

WHO'S YOUR ONE?

Ask someone you trust to be your accountability partner for the rest of *Forgiving Challenge*. Specifically ask them if they'd be able to hear you confess your sins every week and, in response to your confession, offer God's words of forgiveness to you.* Be specific about what you would like this person to do. For instance: Meet weekly, talk/text, ask specific questions, and help when you are struggling. This person needs to be available for periodic check-ins and should be someone with whom you're willing to share your heart. For some, this could be the most difficult of all of the challenges in these 40 days because it requires us to be honest and vulnerable.

* If they need the words to say, this is a common absolution, or declaration of forgiveness:

> *Almighty God in His mercy has given His Son to die for you and for His sake forgives you all your sins. You have been forgiven in the name of the Father, by the blood of the Son, and through the power of the Holy Spirit. Amen.*[47]

ACCOUNTABILITY PARTNER AGREEMENT

Is this person someone I can confess my sins to?

☐ YES   ☐ NO

Is this person someone who can declare God's words of forgiveness to me?*

☐ YES   ☐ NO

Do I trust this person?

☐ YES   ☐ NO

How often will you check in? _____

When will you check in? _____

What are the specific questions you need your accountability partner to ask you?

_____

_____

What would you like this person to do if you're struggling?

_____

_____

19/40

DAYS
20-26
OF THE 40-DAY
CHALLENGE

S.C.A.R.S.

ABSOL

UTION

DAY 20

SURGERY NEEDED

My wife, Allison, grew up on the mission field in West Africa in a small country called Togo. During her time there, she noticed, among some of the tribes, that if a boy stubbed his toe, a friend or the mother would strike the rock that had hurt the child. If a girl fell out of a tree, then her brother would smack the tree. They were trying to set things right by hitting the tree or rock that hurt the other person. But hitting a rock or a tree doesn't make anything right, of course. In our society, we may have a similar reaction if we do something like run into the corner of a table in the dark. We might instinctively slap our hand on the table in anger.

Sometimes, we react in the same ineffective way when we're confronted by sin. When we are hurt by sin, we lash out, sometimes at completely innocent people. Then we brush it off by saying, "I'm having one of those days." We need to invite Jesus into those days.

As we mentioned on Day 2, only 22 percent of American men and 33 percent of American women say they depend on Jesus to overcome sin. This means that the majority of us are trying to find other, creative ways to try to put things right. But the only way to conquer sin is to depend on Jesus.

The process of finding forgiveness and spiritual healing in Jesus can be compared to the healing process for physical injuries, in which wounds turn into scars. This is not always an easy process, and many times it can even be extremely painful.

One of my scariest moments of parenting was right before the Easter season in 2018. My son Brady was seven at the time, and we were hosting a church staff party at our house. The adults were just about ready to eat, and all of the church staff kids were playing outside. As I was praying a blessing over the food, Brady came charging into the house with a type of cry that I had never heard before. It wasn't a loud, piercing cry, but a fear-filled cry. He had been climbing a tree in our backyard, and as he had done hundreds of times before, he jumped down from the tree, expecting to land on his feet. But this particular time, he stumbled as he was jumping. On his fall down the tree, an extremely spiky branch dug into and lacerated his armpit, peeling off a large chunk of skin. Not to get too graphic, but the surgeon would later describe what happened to his armpit as similar to peeling a banana. He had a layer of skin about 5 inches long and 2 inches wide literally just hanging like a banana peel.

Although I struggled because of his pain to get a clear look at what was going on in the moment, I knew this was serious. Brady grew up with an incredibly high pain tolerance, so I knew this was different. I rushed him to the hospital and, amazingly, was greeted by a nurse who attended our church. I didn't need to say anything to her. She knew this was serious just by looking at my face. They took Brady into the emergency room and brought in a surgeon.

Immediately, Brady went into surgery and my wife, Allison, and I were left alone in the lobby of the hospital.

Everything in the couple of hours leading up to this point was a blur to me. Adrenaline had kicked in, and it wasn't until that moment alone in the lobby that I had a little bit of time to process what was going on. But it all started with me and Allison just sitting there with one another, holding each other and crying. It was so hard for us to see our son go through this.

As we were there, I jotted down these words in my notes on my iPhone:

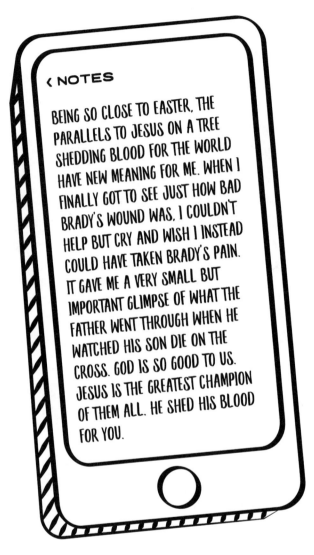

< NOTES

BEING SO CLOSE TO EASTER, THE PARALLELS TO JESUS ON A TREE SHEDDING BLOOD FOR THE WORLD HAVE NEW MEANING FOR ME. WHEN I FINALLY GOT TO SEE JUST HOW BAD BRADY'S WOUND WAS, I COULDN'T HELP BUT CRY AND WISH I INSTEAD COULD HAVE TAKEN BRADY'S PAIN. IT GAVE ME A VERY SMALL BUT IMPORTANT GLIMPSE OF WHAT THE FATHER WENT THROUGH WHEN HE WATCHED HIS SON DIE ON THE CROSS. GOD IS SO GOOD TO US. JESUS IS THE GREATEST CHAMPION OF THEM ALL. HE SHED HIS BLOOD FOR YOU.

I then opened my Bible, and the very first verse that I read filled me with the comfort I needed in a desperate moment:

I AM THE LORD, THE GOD OF ALL MANKIND. IS ANYTHING TOO HARD FOR ME?

- JEREMIAH 32:27

#FORGIVINGCHALLENGE

A couple of hours later, we saw Brady. The surgeon used more than 60 stitches to essentially put the "banana peel" of skin back where it belonged. Those stitches would turn into a pretty killer scar that tells a pretty killer story. Brady not only made a full recovery, but is now using that very same arm to light it up on the Pee-Wee flag football fields!

As painful as the healing was for Brady, part of this process was the surgeon entering into the place where Brady got hurt to ultimately bring healing.

The freedom process that we are undergoing requires similar healing. The process of healing will not be without pain for you, but the most painful part of the healing process has already taken place in the crucifixion of Jesus.

Jesus went to the cross to shed His blood to fulfill the requirements and pay for the sins of the world. Yours, mine, and the whole wide world's. Past, present, and future.

Our week of absolution is about hearing God's declaration of forgiveness over us, and as we enter into it, I want you to most hear His forgiveness in the deepest, darkest, most shame-filled places of your story. You cannot do this on your own. You need Jesus.

Hearing His forgiveness in those deep, dark, shame-filled places will require us to revisit them. When we do, we'll find that this same Jesus who went to the cross to pay the price is unafraid and willing to go back to those painful memories. He will enter into your worst moments with you. Jesus is waiting for you. He's the surgeon you need to heal.

Will you allow Jesus to enter into your worst moments?

CHALLENGE

NOTHING IS TOO HARD

Write this verse from Jeremiah 32:27 three times:

"I am the Lord, the God of all mankind. Is anything too hard for me?"

_____

_____

_____

_____

Do you believe the words in this verse?

_____

What is the hardest thing(s) you need God to do in your life?

_____

When it comes to your sin, what are the deep, dark, shame-filled places that you need the surgeon Jesus to heal?

_____

_____

Do you believe He can bring healing into those places?

_____

20/40

DAY 21

CHARCOAL CHANCES

There's an Indian parable with many variations. One version goes something like this:

There were once six blind men who came upon an elephant for the first time.

- The first man touched the elephant's trunk and said, "This animal is like a snake!"

- The second man touched the tusk and said, "This animal is like a spear!"

- The third man touched the knee and said, "This animal is like a tree!"

- The fourth man touched the ear and said, "This animal is like a fan!"

- The fifth man touched the side of the elephant and said, "This animal is like a wall!"

- The sixth man touched the tail and said, "This animal is like a rope!"

Snake, spear, tree, fan, wall, rope...All very different things. And yet each word described the elephant from that person's point of view. From their points of view, they were each right, but no one was describing the *entire* elephant. This parable teaches us that every one of us can have a different point of view about life, or about a person, event, or sin. Your point of view about your sin has a direct impact on how you receive or understand God's forgiveness.

Point of view also plays an important role in the scene in John 21, the 89th chapter of the Gospels, where Jesus cooks fish on the beach. In this scene, there's an amazing detail that forever changed the way I read the story:

"When they landed, they saw a fire of burning coals there with fish on it, and some bread." John 21:9

While many fires are mentioned throughout the Bible, there are only two places where the Greek word pronounced *an-thrak-i-an*, shows up. Only two. Both of them happen to be in John. This word means "charcoal fire" or "a fire of coals."

The significance of the charcoal fire showing up in #Chapter89 is magnified by the first time we are introduced to this word. It's from John 18:17-18, when a servant girl says:

"'You aren't one of this man's disciples too, are you?' she asked Peter. He replied, 'I am not.'
It was cold, and the servants and officials stood around a fire [*anthrakian*] they had made to keep warm. Peter also was standing with them, warming himself."

It was around a charcoal fire where Peter was at his worst, and not just once. John 18:25-26 records that he denied Jesus a second and third time by that same charcoal fire. After the third denial, just as Jesus had predicted, a rooster crowed. Then Jesus, from a distance, locked eyes with a sorrow-filled Peter.

To truly understand the magnitude of the forgiveness that Jesus is going to offer Peter in John 21, today we are going to attempt to enter Peter's point of view leading up to his exchange with Jesus. Peter is one of the few characters whose story is fully developed in the Bible, so we can make assumptions in which we can be confident.

Peter feels terrible about his denials. Adding to the sorrow of his deeds is the grief of seeing his friend Jesus die. Not only was Peter left to deal with his own failures, but on top of this, he lost someone he desperately loved. At the time when his friend, the one who gave him the opportunity of a lifetime, needed him most, Peter was at his worst.

We're only human, so we naturally replay our worst moments over and over and over again after we fail. I can imagine that Peter's mind kept taking him back to the first charcoal fire, where he denied his Lord. Playing this soundtrack on repeat, the devil spins the guilt into ever-increasing shame. Satan has now convinced Peter that not only did he make a mistake, but he is a failure, a bad friend, a coward, and that he forever ruined an opportunity that will never come his way again.

With the big fisherman now reeling out of control, he suddenly hears the news that Jesus is alive again! He sprints to the tomb to find that it is, in fact, empty! Later that night, with the disciples quarantined in a room out of fear, Jesus bursts through the wall and reveals his nail-scarred hands, thus proving He really is alive!

At this point, I'm sure Peter is a mixed bag of emotions. He's SO excited to see Jesus, but I'm sure he's also SO nervous. He likely has doubts. He starts wondering to himself, *What does Jesus's resurrection mean for me?* He starts reliving other moments he's had with Jesus. He might've been thinking, *I've seen Jesus forgive and grant second chances to others who weren't deserving. Outcasts. Prostitutes. Tax collectors. But I was his right-hand guy. He believed in me. He entrusted His most prized possession, the church, to me. I'm so happy He's alive again, but surely my relationship will be different from here on, right? He could never forgive someone like me, could He?*

As Peter is wallowing in self-doubt, he goes back to fishing. Fishing is what he was confident in. But now he can't even catch fish like he used to. Can he do anything right? At this lowest of points, Jesus shows up on the shore. Not only does He show up in John 21, but as I mentioned before, He recreates the same fish miracle from when He and Peter first met. Jesus also recreates the worst moment of Peter's story, for surely the charcoal fire, the *anthrakian*, reminds Peter of his denials.

I can imagine that doubt immediately creeps in again. *Oh, is that what Jesus is doing?* Peter might've been thinking, *Is He bringing me back to the place where I failed Him? Is He going to tell me He saw what I did? That He's disappointed in me? That I blew the opportunity of a lifetime, and I'll never have it again?*

But this is not what Jesus will do by the fire. Instead, He will have a much-needed conversation with Peter that leads to my personal favorite offering of forgiveness in all of the Bible. When Jesus forgives a criminal hanging next to Him, a wee little chief tax collector named Zacchaeus, a Samaritan woman by a well, or an adulterous woman thrown at His feet, these stories show us that God's forgiveness extends to all people. These stories give us great hope that no matter what we have done, God's grace will cover us!

But Peter's forgiveness story goes to a deeper level. This is Jesus offering forgiveness to His right-hand man, one of His best friends in the whole world. This story gives me hope because if Jesus can forgive someone like Peter, then nothing can stop Him from forgiving someone like me!

So why did Jesus bring Peter back to his worst moment? Was it to rub Peter's face in it, to publicly humiliate him in front of the other disciples? Is it because our God is cruel, and He wants us to feel even worse about ourselves?

This would go against everything the Bible teaches.

The real reason that Jesus brings Peter back to the charcoal fire is not to make Peter relive it, but to *relieve* him of it. Freedom is a painful process, and part of that process is entering into our pain to ultimately bring healing. He recreates the charcoal fire, not because He is a cruel God, but because He is a caring God.

Had this exchange not happened with Jesus, what would be the alternative for Peter? Think about it. Every time a rooster crowed would be a PTSD moment—a "Peter's Traumatic Stress Disorder" moment. Peter would be filled with shame. Guilt. Doubt. Hopelessness. Every fish that Peter caught would put money on the table, but maybe it would also put more regret into his heart, knowing that he failed in the greatest opportunity ever given to him.

Jesus gently reminds Peter in this story: "I have seen you from your first to your worst, and I'm still right by your side today."

God doesn't want us to relive our worst moments. He wants to relieve us from them.

CHALLENGE

INSTANT REPLAYS

What painful moments do you replay over and over again in your story? Do you have one? Two? What does the setting and environment look like? What is your point of view in that moment? Write or draw it in the space below.

Do you believe that Jesus can enter into your worst moments? Explain.

_____

_____

_____

21/40

DAY 22

ZERO BALANCE

One Sunday, Elvina Hall, a long-time churchgoer, widowed mother of three, and musician in her church's choir, sat in her normal place in the church balcony after singing. As the pastor began preaching, her mind wandered off. But rather than thinking about food, football, or family, she pondered the cross, and specifically the meaning of the Greek word *tetelestai*. As we said on Day 3, the word means "it is finished," but it was also an accounting term stamped on receipts that meant "paid in full." As she was pondering this word, she opened up her hymn book and began to write on the flyleaf cover. Afterward, she presented a few simple lines of poetry to the pastor, not telling him when she wrote them!

The pastor, seeing these words, remembered that his organist had just composed a new tune but had no words for it. The pastor then laid the words of Mrs. Hall next to the lines of music and found that her words and the music fit together beautifully! The words and tune have been partners ever since and became the hymn known as "Jesus Paid it All." This hymn has been covered by many notable musicians and gone on to bless tens of millions of people.[48]

I guess not every time that someone nods off in a sermon is a bad thing.

"Jesus paid it all, all to Him I owe," says this hymn. "Sin had left a crimson stain, He washed it white as snow." Fitting words for Peter, as he gathered with Jesus around the charcoal fire. This is the moment when Peter experiences Jesus paying it all for him.

"When they had finished eating, Jesus said to Simon Peter, 'Simon son of John, do you love me more than these?'

"'Yes, Lord,' he said, 'you know that I love you.'

"Jesus said, 'Feed my lambs.'

"Again Jesus said, 'Simon son of John, do you love me?'

"He answered, 'Yes, Lord, you know that I love you.'

"Jesus said, 'Take care of my sheep.'

"The third time he said to him, 'Simon son of John, do you love me?'

"Peter was hurt because Jesus asked him the third time, 'Do you love me?' He said, 'Lord, you know all things; you know that I love you.'

"Jesus said, 'Feed my sheep.'" John 21:15-17

Jesus asks Peter three times, **"Do you love me?"**

We'll dive into the meaning of these questions and answers soon, but for today I simply want to point out an obvious fact. The number of questions that Jesus asked Peter is the same number of times that Peter had failed—three. For Jesus to fully absolve Peter, He took Peter through the same question three times to demonstrate that all three of Peter's denials were taken care of. He gave Peter three opportunities to say the right thing by the charcoal fire after he had said the wrong thing three times prior at a different charcoal fire.

When it comes to forgiveness, God doesn't want you to hang onto your sin, stuff away your sin, or suppress your sin. He doesn't want or need you to try to overcome your sin by yourself. But He will ask you to go backward to examine your sin before He will invite you to move forward with His grace.

If we don't go back and reconcile all of the ways in which we've failed Him, we will not be as effective for Him as we can be in the future. When we don't allow God to fully absolve us from all of our past mistakes, we drag our mistakes and failures along with us. It's no wonder that in our pursuit to move forward, we aren't living effectively. We're carrying all of this baggage around with us.

Again, God's endgame is not that the cobwebs would be cleaned out, but that your spider would be killed. This will allow you to live a life where you are totally free from your sin and totally free to be the person He's called you to be.

Maybe an illustration from the accounting world will help you fully grasp this concept.

A couple of years ago, as I started my new business, I decided to be in charge of my own bookkeeping. I had always been pretty good with numbers, and I thought it would be easy for me. I entered into a world I didn't know much about. There were multiple tax forms that nobody shared with me that needed to be filled out quarterly and annually. On top of that, I had to create a list of all expenses, categorize them appropriately, track revenue, etc., to create profit-and-loss statements. Although it took me many months to figure it out, I felt like I was finally hitting my stride. I showed my books to a tax accountant, and she told me, "Wow, you are doing a really great job at keeping up." I felt very proud of myself—until tax time came.

I thought I had everything ready for taxes. I did what everybody told me I needed to do up to that point. However, at the end of the year, my tax accountant suddenly said, "Everything looks good. Now, in order to finish your year-end taxes, we'll just need you to fully reconcile your accounts. You need to make sure they all end with a zero balance."

Wait, what? This was an extremely tedious process, but thankfully, with everything done online these days, I was able to import balance sheets and transactions. When a problem showed up, I'd figure out how to make it right, or why an error occurred.

The process ended up taking days, and I almost got there completely. *Almost.* One account still had a $30 difference, and my accountant said, "No, you can't have a $30 difference. You need to have it perfectly balanced at $0."

So, I was forced to comb through every transaction. But no matter how hard I looked, I couldn't find the error. I then printed out page after page of every transaction. I checked not only the dollar amounts but the transaction ID's to make sure they were all imported carefully. It felt like a major waste of time. I called my accountant and said, "Listen it's only $30. Can I just write you a check for $30, and you can make this go away? I've looked at every transaction, and I give up!" She said, "No, but how about if I take a look for you?" I gave her permission, and the next day she called me and said, "I found it!"

Apparently, even though every transaction ID number that I checked was pulled in perfectly to my accounting software, for some reason one of the automatically imported transactions pulled in $28 instead of $58. "There's your $30 difference," she said. She also explained that in the accounting world, it's rare, but every now and then technology's automated imports pull in the wrong number. The technology may be right 99.9 percent of the time, but 0.1 percent of the time, it'll be a little bit off.

This small glitch made me hesitant to trust fully in technology. I began worrying about the technology leading us into a future with self-driving cars! In a car, we kind of need things to be right 100 percent of the time, not 99.9 percent, right?

But in this painful process of going back and reconciling all of the numbers, I learned the beautiful art of getting to the zero balance. By getting to a zero balance, I could now move forward without any of the past transactions entering into my future.

Jesus has perfectly reconciled you. You can now move forward without any of your past mistakes dragging you down. Jesus asks Peter three times for Peter to be fully reconciled. This allows Peter to move forward without his past haunting him or holding him back. Jesus balanced the books.

I like how Mike Foster talks about this in his book *Freeway*: "Two thousand years ago, a rooster crowed, and a man took on all of the world's injustice, filth, abuse, and rottenness and said, '*Tetelestai*.' And with that, forgiveness wins, and the elusive chase is over."[49]

CHALLENGE

JESUS PAID IT ALL

Your challenge today is to read the words of the hymn, "Jesus Paid it All." Then, much like Mrs. Hall wrote in the margin of her hymn book, write what words come to your mind as you read these lyrics. As a bonus, feel free to listen to the song "Jesus Paid it All" as you read and write.

I hear the savior say,
"Thy strength indeed is small;
Child of weakness, watch and pray,
Find in Me thine all in all."

Chorus: Jesus paid it all,
All to him I owe;
Sin had left a crimson stain,
He washed it white as snow.

Lord, now indeed I find
Thy power and thine alone,
Can change the leper's spots
And melt the heart of stone.

Chorus

And when before the throne,
I stand in him complete,
Jesus died my soul to save,
My lips shall still repeat.

Chorus

(The words of the bridge
were added later:)

Oh, praise the one who paid my debt
And raises life up from the dead.
Oh, praise the one who paid my debt
And raises life up from the dead.
Oh, praise the one who paid my debt
And raises life up from the dead.

22/40

DAY 23

PHILE-O-FISH

I know it is absolution week, but I still have a confession to make. At 37 years old, I just ate my first McRib sandwich.

I know I shouldn't have. I know many of you are judging me for it, because, well, I had previously judged others before me who ate a McRib. I don't understand how this conglomeration of meat is shaped like a rib, tastes like a rib, and yet somehow has no bones. It is pork, as far as I know, but it's not a rib, is it? It's confusing. But it's delicious! In fact, I'll go ahead and say it, "I love the McRib!"

Love...Our English language doesn't do us much justice with the word "love."

Using the same word, we can profess our love for a McRib, and I can profess my love for my wife. Eve, the world's first spouse, may have come from Adam's rib. But clearly, hopefully, there is a different type of love that you and I would have for our spouse than for a McRib!

Does the word "love" lose its meaning when it is used in so many ways?

In the Greek, there are four different words for love. "Agape" and "phileo" were the two used the most often. Agape refers to an unconditional love, a love that goes beyond a feeling; it's a love that is there not just in the good times, but the bad as well. Agape love also has the connotation of a love that requires sacrifice. The most famous wedding passage, 1 Corinthians 13:4-13—the one that starts by saying, "Love is patient, love is kind..."— is referring to an agape love. God's love for us is most commonly thought of us agape love. God loves us unconditionally, sacrificially, at all times no matter what.

Phileo refers to an affectionate, or brotherly, love. That's why the city of Philadelphia is known as the city of brotherly love. This is the type of love that close friends have for one another. It is a companionable and relational type of love.

The reason I bring this up is because in the exchange between Jesus and Peter, both types of love are mentioned. Let's take another look at John 21:15-17:

> **"When they had finished eating, Jesus said to Simon Peter, 'Simon son of John, do you AGAPE love me more than these?'**
>
> **"'Yes, Lord,' he said, 'you know that I PHILEO love you.'**
>
> **"Jesus said, 'Feed my lambs.'**
>
> **"Again Jesus said, 'Simon son of John, do you AGAPE love me?'**
>
> **"He answered, 'Yes, Lord, you know that I PHILEO love you.'**
>
> **"Jesus said, 'Take care of my sheep.'**
>
> **"The third time he said to him, 'Simon son of John, do you PHILEO love me?'**
>
> **"Peter was hurt because Jesus asked him the third time, 'Do you PHILEO love me?' He said, 'Lord, you know all things; you know that I PHILEO love you.'**
>
> **"Jesus said, 'Feed my sheep.'"**

Did you notice that in the first two instances Jesus used the word agape and yet Peter returned with phileo? Finally, asking for the third time, Jesus changes to phileo. In this instance, we can see that Peter was hurt. But even while grieving, he responds back with a phileo declaration of love.

Scholars are widely split on the meaning of this. Some scholars believe there is much significance. They teach that through this questioning, Peter realizes he hasn't yet fully matured to agape love, and he is sad that Jesus had to come down to his level and settle for a friendship type of love instead.

Other scholars teach that there is nothing to glean from this change in words. They will then point out how interchangeably John uses these two words for love throughout his entire Gospel.

As the debate between scholars continues, it's possible that the answer to why Jesus did this is less theological and more practical. Sometimes, it simply takes repetition to drive home a point.

Even if we know we are guilty, it is still never easy to be confronted with our sin. Just this week, I caught one of my boys snatching some Twizzlers from the pantry. They were clearly told no more Twizzlers for the rest of the day. I knew he had done this deed, but he didn't know that I knew.

I asked him, "Do you have anything you need to tell me?"

"No dad, I'm good. You good?"

I asked him a second time, "You sure you don't have anything to tell me?

"Nothing I can think of...Do you have anything you need to tell me, Dad?"

I asked him a third time. "One last time, are you sure you don't have anything to tell me?" This time, though, I raised my voice an octave and hung onto the word "anything" a bit longer. I may have also been holding a Twizzler in my hand.

Boom! Something about the third question brought about the confession that allowed me to forgive him. While we can laugh at kids snatching Twizzlers, we do the same thing. We sin and we hide. When we are confronted with sin, the devil always urges us to keep on denying it. Sometimes it takes the same question, rephrased slightly different, for us to snap out of this denial.

The reality is that no matter what type of love—agape or phileo—Peter failed Jesus in both. He'd been filled with sorrow since the moment Jesus locked eyes with him by the first charcoal fire. If agape love is unconditional and sacrificial, Peter's cowardly actions by the first charcoal fire fell way short. If phileo love is the love that a friend or companion has for one another, he also got it wrong because friends don't abandon friends in their deepest time of need.

At the root of it, a lot of people who profess to love Jesus, including yours truly, mess up. And when we hear, when we see, when we taste the goodness of God in spite of our sin, we feel badly that we let him down. But the reality is that Jesus didn't bring Peter back to the charcoal fire so that he could right his wrongs. It wasn't like Peter said "No" three times by the first charcoal fire, so Jesus needed him to say "Yes" three times by the second charcoal fire to make it right. That's not how God's forgiveness works.

Jesus doesn't need Peter to right any wrongs. Jesus did all of that at the cross.

What Peter needed by the fire was to be reminded that even in his failure to agape and phileo Jesus, the Lord never failed to agape and phileo him. What you need to be reminded of today is that God doesn't need you to right all of your wrongs. He's already paid the price in full for you. Jesus agape's you. Jesus phileo's you. You are forgiven.

Look at how David shares this truth with us in Psalm 103:12:

"...as far as the east is from the west, so far has he removed our transgressions from us."

You don't need to be a Hebrew scholar to understand that "as far as the east is from the west" equals all of the sins of all people of all time, including Peter's.

Hear it, see it, taste it.

As much as the McRib may satisfy a craving, it's the "Phile-O-Fish" that God is cooking up for breakfast and offers to Peter. This is the meal that truly satisfies our soul.

CHALLENGE

EAST TO WEST

Read Psalm 103. In this Psalm, we see that God has removed every sin from east to west. Underline important verses and journal key thoughts on the side as you read through this powerful Psalm.

Praise the Lord, my soul;
    all my inmost being, praise his holy name.
Praise the Lord, my soul,
    and forget not all his benefits—
who forgives all your sins
    and heals all your diseases,
who redeems your life from the pit
    and crowns you with love and compassion,
who satisfies your desires with good things
    so that your youth is renewed like
    the eagle's.

The Lord works righteousness
    and justice for all the oppressed.

He made known his ways to Moses,
    his deeds to the people of Israel:
The Lord is compassionate and gracious,
    slow to anger, abounding in love.
He will not always accuse,
    nor will he harbor his anger forever;
he does not treat us as our sins deserve
    or repay us according to our iniquities.
For as high as the heavens are above the
earth,
    so great is his love for those who fear him;
as far as the east is from the west,
    so far has he removed our transgressions
    from us.

As a father has compassion on his children,
    so the Lord has compassion on those
    who fear him;
for he knows how we are formed,
    he remembers that we are dust.
The life of mortals is like grass,
    they flourish like a flower of the field;
the wind blows over it and it is gone,
    and its place remembers it no more.
But from everlasting to everlasting
    the Lord's love is with those who fear him,
    and his righteousness with their children's
    children—
with those who keep his covenant
    and remember to obey his precepts.

The Lord has established his throne in heaven,
    and his kingdom rules over all.

Praise the Lord, you his angels,
    you mighty ones who do his bidding,
    who obey his word.
Praise the Lord, all his heavenly hosts,
    you his servants who do his will.
Praise the Lord, all his works
    everywhere in his dominion.

Praise the Lord, my soul.

23/40

DAY 24

KAI PETRO

2020 was the year when everything was turned upside down. As a result of the coronavirus pandemic, people's first response was to hoard toilet paper. Weird, right? Major industries were wiped out, work was forced into the home, jobs were lost, and church buildings were shut down for Easter. The Cleveland Browns had a winning football season. Nothing was the same.

Even the way we viewed characters in a classic good vs. evil movie like *The Karate Kid* began to change.

The Karate Kid instantly became a classic in 1984. Daniel LaRusso was the underdog we all loved to root for. This scrawny, New Jersey, fatherless transplant had just moved to California. As hard as it is to acclimate into a new high school as a teenager, what made it even harder was that he ran into the ultimate bully named Johnny Lawrence. Eventually, Daniel's neighbor, Mr. Miyagi, who happened to be a karate sensei, empathized with Daniel and began teaching him how to defend himself against bullies. Mr. Miyagi would teach Daniel that karate was for self-defense, and he used unique training tactics like cleaning fences, scrubbing cars ("wax on, wax off"), and trimming bonsai trees. Through Mr. Miyagi's leadership, Daniel quickly turned into a great fighter.

Meanwhile, Johnny Lawrence was the prized student of sensei John Kreese in the Cobra Kai dojo. However, Kreese didn't teach karate for self-defense, but rather, as a way to dominate and assert your authority in this world. The motto that he taught his students: "Strike first. Strike hard. No mercy." And nobody was better at striking first, striking hard, and showing no mercy than Johnny Lawrence.

The movie ends with Daniel LaRusso defeating the evil Johnny Lawrence. Ever since the movie hit the big screen, it has been pretty clear-cut. We were taught to love Daniel LaRusso, the good guy, and hate Johnny Lawrence, the bad guy.

Then 2020 came. Thanks to the Netflix show, *Cobra Kai*, 73 million households were re-introduced to the story, and many began to soften their feelings about the karate dojo, Cobra Kai, and its main character, Johnny Lawrence.[50]

Through the new series, viewers were let in on Johnny's backstory. And somehow, strangely, many found themselves in a conundrum, not sure if they should root for Johnny, for Daniel, or for both. Even though Johnny is crude, rude, and terribly offensive, the show depicts just enough redeeming qualities in him that many ultimately began cheering for him in the end.

However, isn't that how things are? The more we dive into someone's story, the more we begin to empathize with them. While it still doesn't make the person's sin right, many times it can soften our harsh stance toward them.

As the world was swept into the madness of *Cobra Kai*, it was another "Kai" that started getting my attention in 2020. Did you know that in Greek, the word for "and" is pronounced "*kai*"? The particular instance of *kai* that blows me away is found in Mark 16:7, directly after the resurrection of Jesus. On that Sunday morning, three women, Mary Magdalene, Mary the mother of James, and Salome, went to the tomb to embalm the body of Jesus. Expecting to find Jesus, they were instead greeted by an angel. Not only did the angel comfort the women with the announcement that Jesus had risen, but then the angel gave them a special command:

"But go, tell his disciples and Peter, 'He is going ahead of you into Galilee. There you will see him, just as he told you.'" Mark 16:7

Did you see it? The angel said, "The disciples AND Peter." The disciples *kai* Petro. Jesus distinguishes Peter from the rest.

What does this show us? In the course of the grand rescue mission for all people, Jesus put Peter's freedom opportunity at the forefront of His rescue. This friend of His, to whom He had entrusted so much and empowered with such a high calling, was still on the mind of Jesus! The angel says to tell all of the disciples, which means that every single one will be offered grace, forgiveness, and an invitation to follow Jesus again. But He also singles out Peter. God has special forgiveness, special hope, and a special opportunity for Peter.

I love what Charles Spurgeon says about this verse:

"If any of you have behaved worse to your Master than others, you are peculiarly called to come to him now. You have grieved him, and you have been grieving because you have grieved him. You have been brought to repentance after having slidden away from him, and now he seals your pardon by inviting you to himself."[51]

Don't you see how far our God will go to get back what is His? Don't you see how loving and kind our God is to allow chance after chance after chance to us?

If He did this for Peter, He can do it for you. If He can hunt down, chase, and forgive Peter, He can hunt down, chase, and forgive you. You are on the mind of Jesus. You are included in the total redemption of all people.

How amazing that in the midst of this rescue story and mission, in which Jesus will bring freedom to all, He is also able to have a singular focus on the "one."

Jesus doesn't fight the way we fight. Rather than attacking, He gives us grace. Rather than teaching us self-defense, He became our defense. Instead of Strike First, Strike Hard, No Mercy, Jesus battles with this motto: Serve First, Serve Hard, Show Mercy.

Jesus fought the ultimate fight for you so you would stop fighting yourself. His declaration and full payment of sins includes the whole world. And (kai) it includes you.

CHALLENGE

AND YOU

Read the resurrection account of Mark 16:1-7:

"When the Sabbath was over, Mary Magdalene, Mary the mother of James, and Salome bought spices so that they might go to anoint Jesus' body. Very early on the first day of the week, just after sunrise, they were on their way to the tomb and they asked each other, 'Who will roll the stone away from the entrance of the tomb?'

"But when they looked up, they saw that the stone, which was very large, had been rolled away. As they entered the tomb, they saw a young man dressed in a white robe sitting on the right side, and they were alarmed.

"'Don't be alarmed,' he said. 'You are looking for Jesus the Nazarene, who was crucified. He has risen! He is not here. See the place where they laid him. But go, tell his disciples and Peter, "He is going ahead of you into Galilee. There you will see him, just as he told you."'"

If Jesus said "and Peter" (*kai Petro*) on that Easter morning, He also says to me, "and Zach" (*kai Zach*). He says your name too. In fact, go ahead and write it:

"AND _____."

Do you believe Jesus's rescue mission for the whole world includes rescuing you? Why or why not?

_____

_____

_____

_____

_____

_____

_____

_____

_____

_____

_____

24/40

DAY 25

#NAILEDIT

Gary Chapman wrote a wildly successful and helpful book called *The Five Love Languages*. The premise of the book is that people prefer to receive love in one of five ways: words of affirmation, quality time, acts of service, physical touch, or receiving gifts. In December 2010, Chapman created an online quiz and found that the most common primary love language is, in fact, words of affirmation.[52]

Words of affirmation happens to be my primary love language—although I would argue for a sixth love language simply called "food." The way to this man's heart is through his stomach. Amen.

At different points of our lives, we are desperate to hear certain words. One of my favorite little books (and by little, I mean *really* little) is John Eldredge's book *You Have What It Takes: What Every Father Needs to Know.* In this book, Eldredge makes the case that the words that a father speaks to his children are of utmost importance. Having the privilege of being a father of two sons, I want to make sure I'm saying the right words to them. Eldredge makes the case that every son desperately wants to hear these words from his father: "You have what it takes." Every daughter is waiting to hear these three words: "You are lovely." These words, spoken over and over to our children, can help shape and mold them into the people God is calling them to be.

I still remember words from decades ago that I carry with me. I remember a word of encouragement that my youth pastor spoke over me when I was in high school that still encourages me today. I remember a word of discouragement a professor spoke over me at college that hurt me. Sticks and stones may in fact break our bones, but words are capable of sticking daggers in our heart.

As important as continual words of affirmation might be, the three words you need to hear to ultimately become free are these three powerful words: "I forgive you."

Last week, as we explored confession, we noted that we never actually heard, read, or saw the words "I'm sorry" from Peter. Jesus looked past the words and could see straight into Peter's heart. This week, I want to point out that nowhere in the charcoal-fire conversation do we hear, read, or see the words "I forgive you" from Jesus. We made the case last week that we'll make again today: This story is deeper than words. There's so much in the meaning and context: recreating the first fish miracle, the fact that Jesus is cooking breakfast, the fact that the breakfast is over a charcoal fire, and the significance of the three denials paired with the three questions by Jesus.

The truth, however, is that Jesus didn't need to have this specific conversation with Peter for Peter to be forgiven. Jesus had already said the words "I forgive you." And Peter, although at a distance, had already heard Jesus say these words while the Lord hung on the cross:

"Father, forgive them, for they know not what they are doing." Luke 23:34a

The "them" not only included the ones who were physically responsible for creating the scars on the hands of Jesus, but it included Peter, and it includes you and me. This was a once-and-for-all absolution declaration.

On Day 11, we read about the rigorous process the high priest would have to undergo to atone and pay for his sins, and the sins of all of the people. Hebrews

10:11 says, **"Day after day every priest stands and performs his religious duties; again and again he offers the same sacrifices, which can never take away sins."**

Then, on Day 16, we read about how the sacrifice of Jesus was the single sacrifice needed for all of humankind. His death on the cross, combined with the subsequent tearing of the curtain, was an announcement that all sins for all people of all time had been atoned.

This is confirmed for us in Hebrews 10:12-14:

> **"But when this priest had offered for all time one sacrifice for sins, he sat down at the right hand of God, and since that time he waits for his enemies to be made his footstool. For by one sacrifice he has made perfect forever those who are being made holy."**

The cross is really big. It was *the* sacrifice to pay for all sins of all people. But included in this BIG sacrifice is you and me. Your sins and my sins. Jesus not only paid the price for the sins of the whole world, but He also paid for your sins. Knowing all of this, we can say with confidence that the absolution declaration, **"Father, forgive them,"** includes the words "I forgive you" to Peter and "I forgive you" to you. The absolution declaration on the cross is all that Peter needed to hear. Jesus had already said the words, and He paid a big cost when He spoke them. That had to stick with Peter forever.

It's one thing to hear "I forgive you" when the one forgiving you didn't have to pay a great cost. For instance, if my son steals $1 from my overall net worth, that's an easy cost for me to absorb. But what if my son did something that came at a great

JESUS NOT ONLY
PAID THE PRICE
FOR THE SINS OF
THE WHOLE WORLD,
BUT HE ALSO PAID
FOR YOUR SINS.

#FORGIVINGCHALLENGE

cost to me? If my son could see the pain and consequence of his action and yet still hear me say, "I forgive you," that will stick with him forever.

Peter didn't need to hear the words "I forgive you" by the charcoal fire because he already heard the words at Jesus's most painful moment on the cross. In hearing the words, he not only got to see just how serious his sin was, but also how much greater God's grace is.

This 40-day challenge started with the idea of the nail-scarred hands of Jesus bringing the opportunity of freedom to all of us. But did you know that the nails that went through the hands and feet of Jesus were not the only nails used in the crucifixion story?

The soldiers in charge of his crucifixion also nailed a sign above his head that read, "King of the Jews." But as they were using nails to hang a man and a sign upon a cross, Jesus was nailing something else to the cross that day. Look at how J.B. Phillips translates Colossians 2:13-14:

> **"He has forgiven you all your sins: Christ has utterly wiped out the damning evidence of broken laws and commandments which always hung over our heads, and has completely annulled it by nailing it over his own head on the cross."**

Jesus nailed all sin on the cross. May the declaration that Jesus says over you yesterday, today, tomorrow, and forever—"I forgive you"—be forever nailed to your heart.

CHALLENGE

WORDS OF SIGNIFICANCE

What positive words spoken to you have stuck with you for a long time? Who spoke them, and why do you still remember them?

_____

_____

What negative words spoken to you have stuck with you for a long time and why? Who spoke them, and why do you still remember them?

_____

_____

Are there any words that you wished someone would say to you today? What are those words, and why do you need to hear them? What difference would those words make in your life today?

_____

_____

Write the words "I forgive you. Love, God." on a sheet of paper, sticky note, or white board. Then put it in a prominent place in your house.

25/40

DAY 26

WHY CAN'T I FORGIVE MYSELF?

Forgiving other people who have wronged us is one of the hardest commands of Jesus. But what if the person whom you feel most wronged, betrayed, and let down by is yourself? Is it possible to forgive yourself?

Most people have a harder time forgiving themselves than forgiving others. In doing research upon writing this book, I posed the question to my social media friends:

"Is it harder to forgive yourself or others? Explain."

Almost unanimously, the results came back that it was harder to forgive themselves than to forgive others.

Levi Lusko writes, "I have no doubt that the devil sends demons to mess with me, and the world might very well be another source of problems that come at me. But this I know for sure: I cause more than enough problems to keep myself occupied. The three sources of my primary frustration in life are as follows: me, myself, and I."[53]

As people explained their answers, one of the responses really stuck out to me: "Is forgiving yourself even a biblical principle? How important is self-forgiveness after all?"

When facing big theological questions like this, my first response is to look to Jesus. What did Jesus say?

Not only did Jesus never use the phrases "forgive myself" or "forgive yourself," but nowhere in the Bible do we see these words together. However, we do see Him asking, calling, encouraging, and even commanding His followers to forgive others. Here are only a few instances:

- In the Lord's Prayer, Jesus says we are to pray these words: **"And forgive us our debts, as we also have forgiven our debtors." Matthew 6:12**

- In teaching the disciples, Jesus said: **"And when you stand praying, if you hold anything against anyone, forgive them, so that your Father in heaven may forgive you your sins." Mark 11:25**

- In directly addressing Peter: **"Then Peter came to Jesus and asked, 'Lord, how many times shall I forgive my brother or sister who sins against me? Up to seven times?' Jesus answered, 'I tell you, not seven times, but seventy-seven times.'" Matthew 18:21-22**

What do we make of all of this?

It's clear that Jesus calls us to forgive others. But typically, there is a direct correlation between receiving God's forgiveness first for ourselves, and then being able to forgive others. If we struggle to forgive others, the root of it may be that we struggle to grasp God's forgiveness for ourselves.

Sometimes the "other" that most needs forgiveness is yourself.

Therefore, even though the phrase "forgive myself" is not found in the Bible, it is a biblical principle because Jesus is all about the total forgiveness of all of people, and you are included in that.

If Jesus has declared forgiveness over all of your sins, why then do you struggle to forgive yourself? I'm going to give you an answer that not many are telling you, and you probably won't like it. The ultimate reason you struggle to forgive yourself is because you are still sinful.

Because Jesus has forgiven you, then you ought to be able to forgive yourself. When you refuse to forgive anyone, including yourself, you are sinning. You are simply adding sin upon sin, and that holds so many back from living the free, abundant life that Jesus offers.

Even after your sins are wiped clean, fully paid, reconciled, and declared forgiven, we still live in a world where we miss the mark. We may claim to be following Jesus as our Lord, but sin still lurks all around us, and, sadly, we often give in to those temptations. One of the ways we still miss the mark today is when we refuse to issue forgiveness to others and to ourselves.

The two most common types of sin lurking behind an unwillingness to forgive ourselves are pride and unbelief.

PRIDE comes into the equation when you place yourself in a higher category than Jesus. The phrase often said is: "I know Jesus forgives me, but I can't forgive myself." As I said earlier, this phrase may sound self-deprecating, but it is laced with pride. Do you really think that your own forgiveness is the ultimate forgiveness you can attain? Do you place your own declaration of forgiveness higher than Jesus's declaration of forgiveness for you? Pride places you at a level you were never meant to be. You are important and valuable in God's kingdom, but you are not more important, valuable, or higher than God's one and only Son, Jesus! You need to lower your estimation of yourself.

UNBELIEF comes through statements like this: "Jesus might be able forgive someone like them, but He can't forgive what I've done." Do you think that your sin is in a special category of sins? Are there certain types of sin that Jesus didn't pay for at the cross? The reality is that Jesus paid in full for all sins for all people for all time, including yours. Being unable to forgive your own sin is to express an unbelief in the sacrifice, death, resurrection, and total defeat of sin that Jesus endured.

Have you done stupid things? Yes.

Did you let Jesus down? Yes.

Did you even let yourself down? Yes.

Do you believe that Jesus has forgiven you? Yes or No?

Ask it again but make it personal this time: Do I believe that Jesus has forgiven me? Yes or No?

If you do, then why are you still making yourself pay for your sin? Why are you rejecting God's forgiveness? Why are you buying into the lie that your sin(s) isn't covered?

If you don't believe your sin is covered, then keep coming back to the charcoal fire story of Jesus and Peter. See the ways, the lengths, and the depths that Jesus went to in order to help one person come to an understanding of his brokenness. As you see Jesus doing this in the life of Peter, know that Jesus has gone, is going, and will go just as far for you. He loves you that much!

It is my belief that followers of Jesus have a long way to go when it comes to forgiving others. Collectively, we have not been known for grace, but rather, our reputation is the opposite—judgment. It'll always be hard to bring freedom to others when we are still speaking words of condemnation over ourselves.

We are called to forgive others as Jesus has forgiven us. The first "other" you need to forgive is yourself.

FORGIVE YOURSELF

Say the words, "I forgive you, _____ (fill in your name)." Then read the following paragraph and write these words in the space allotted on the next page.

Jesus forgives me. Jesus paid the price for all sins of all people of all time, including my past, present, and future sins. Jesus gives me a free gift called grace. I cannot earn it, and I never will deserve it. He just gives it to me. Because of this gift of grace, I choose to forgive myself. I choose to let go of my past sins that have kept me in bondage so that I can walk forward in freedom. I will not continue to pay a price that God does not ask me to pay. I will let the blood of Jesus cover my sins. I will let His declaration of forgiveness for the entire world include me in it.

_____

_____

_____

_____

_____

_____

_____

_____

_____

_____

_____

_____

_____

Yesterday you wrote the words, "I forgive you. Love, God." and displayed those words in a prominent place in your house. Today, write the words, "If God has forgiven you, I forgive you too, _(insert your name)._" Then place these words in the same prominent place in your house.

26/40

DAYS
27-33

OF THE 40-DAY

CHALLENGE

S.C.A.R.S.

RESTO

RATION

DAY 27

THE KINGDOM IS AVAILABLE

Congratulations! You made it to restoration week!

This is the week we are going to start to see how all of the pieces fit back together. That is ultimately what restoration is about. It's about bringing something back to its original state. However, because God is a master restorer, He doesn't just put things back to their original condition. He brings them back to something even more beautiful, effective, and glorious.

Before we jump back into the powerful story of Jesus forgiving Peter, I want to take a broader look at God's ultimate desire for full restoration.

Many people have a false assumption that the ultimate goal of Christianity is to come to a relationship with Jesus Christ so that when you die you can go to heaven. If that were the end goal, then you could stop at Day 26 in *Forgiving Challenge.*

Make no mistake about it: It will be a glorious day, moment, and eternity when we finally see Jesus in heaven! I love the promise of Romans 8:18: **"I consider that our present sufferings are not worth comparing with the glory that will be revealed in us."** Far more often, however, Jesus focuses *not* on escaping this world so one day we go up in the clouds to heaven, but on bringing heaven down to earth.

In *Red Letter Challenge*, I encouraged people to read and do the words of Jesus (the red letters). After reading through all of the commands that Jesus gave to His disciples, I located five targets to become a great follower of Jesus: Being,

Forgiving, Serving, Giving, and Going. While my previous book was primarily focused on looking at the commands of Jesus, if you were to look at the entirety of all that Jesus said, all of His red letters, He spoke far more on the subject of the Kingdom of God than anything else. The very first documented words of His public ministry are found in Matthew 4:17b (ESV): **"Repent, for the kingdom of heaven is at hand."** The Greek word *eggiken* usually is translated as "at hand" or "has come near." It is a verb form indicating a past and completed action.

Dallas Willard says in *The Divine Conspiracy*, "This kingdom is not something to be 'accepted' now and enjoyed later, but something to be *entered* now. It is something that already has flesh-and-blood citizens who have been transformed into it and are fellow workers in it."[54]

The central message that Jesus came to announce was that the Kingdom of Heaven is available to all—*now*. It had always been available prior to Jesus, but His arrival, coming down from heaven to earth, brought new accessibility. The light coming into the darkness brought this reality to life like never before seen.

While God's kingdom is at hand now, there are other kingdoms at work now as well. This is ultimately why we are still struggling to be free. There is still a spiritual battle raging as we speak. Just as there is a "now" aspect to God's kingdom, there is also a "not yet" aspect to fully seeing God's restored kingdom. Ultimately, that is why Jesus urges us to pray these words in the Lord's Prayer, found in Matthew 6:10 (NASB): **"Thy kingdom come. Thy will be done, on earth as it is in heaven."**

N.T. Wright said in his groundbreaking book, *Surprised by Hope*, "Jesus's resurrection is the beginning of God's new project not to snatch people away from earth to heaven but to colonize earth with the life of heaven. That, after all, is what the Lord's Prayer is all about."[55]

Jesus came to announce His kingdom, to reveal what His kingdom looks like, and through His resurrection to show us that His kingdom will be victorious.

He was far more interested in renewing, recreating, and restoring this world, not in blowing it up and destroying it. We see this in the overall scope of what Jesus said, His words in the Lord's Prayer, and also in the revelation of John in the final two chapters of our Bible. From beginning to end, the Bible is about God's full restoration of the world, of which humanity is an integral piece of the entire puzzle.

When you think about God restoring the entire world, it gives you an entirely different perspective and approach to life today. It means that we can not only enter into that kingdom through the blood of Jesus, but now we can participate in it as well. What we do in this world does in fact matter. Someone once asked the great reformer, Martin Luther, what he would do if he knew that Jesus was coming back today. Luther responded that he would plant a tree. Why? Because if God is about full restoration, then the little things we do in this world matter. His belief is that somehow in the new, fully restored kingdom of God, the tree that he planted would be utilized, loved, and give even more glory to God.

Until Christ returns again, we would do well to play our part in His total restoration of the whole world. Again, we return to words from N.T. Wright:

> "The point of the resurrection…is that the present bodily life is not valueless just because it will die…What you do in the present—by painting, preaching, singing, sewing, praying, teaching, building hospitals, digging wells, campaigning for justice, writing poems, caring for the needy, loving your neighbor as yourself—will last into God's future. These activities are not simply ways of making the present life a little less beastly, a little more bearable, until the day when we leave it behind altogether…They are part of what we may call building for God's kingdom."[56]

CHALLENGE

HEAVEN TO EARTH

God's ultimate desire is the full restoration of this world. Amazingly, God has created us in His image. And if He is the Master restorer, we are His mini-restorers in this world. Because we are made in God's image, when Jesus prays, **"Thy kingdom come. Thy will be done, on earth as it is in heaven,"** we get to be a part of bringing heaven to earth today in some way.

As you look at your life—the people, circumstances, and community in which you live—list five areas, things, or people that you believe need God's restoration.

1 _____

2 _____

3 _____

4 _____

5 _____

How can you bring heaven to earth in the above areas?

Your challenge today is to restore or start restoring one of the five areas mentioned above.

What did you do? Share on social media using #ForgivingChallenge.

27/40

DAY 28

JESUS THE RESTORER

I loved garage sales as a child. These were my first ventures into the entrepreneurial world. A few months ago, I realized that because of technological platforms introduced in the last couple of decades, such as eBay, Craig's List, and Facebook Marketplace, my sons had never gone through a proper garage sale. It was time to change that! We signed our family up for the next community-wide garage sale.

My kids learned an important lesson that day. Stuff is worth only as much as someone is willing to pay. This was a lesson I learned not only at garage sales, but also in my younger days of buying, trading, and selling sports cards. Even though *Beckett* magazine might tell me my Ken Griffey, Jr.'s Upper Deck rookie card was worth $100, if someone was only willing to pay $10 for it, that's all it was worth.

At the end of our garage sale, we sold most of our stuff for pennies on the dollar.

Isn't that true for stuff in general? Almost all of our stuff loses value. Your purchase may feel valuable in the moment, but eventually it loses value. You will either sell it at a garage sale for $2, give it to a charity, or throw it away a decade later at a dump. But you could also explore a fourth option. You could figure out a way to restore the item so that it still has great value for use in the future.

I've had the privilege for the last decade to live in Mount Dora, Florida, home to the world famous Renninger's Antique Marketplaces. I've gotten to know the Renninger family (we've even hosted large church events on their property) and have been really impressed with their business. Their marketplace is filled with shops and vendors who are masterful at restoring and repurposing things that you or I might have passed over. They take things of the past and restore them to make them useful for the future.

Why are we spending so much time today discussing garage sales, baseball cards, and antiques? What does this have to do with our freedom experience?

Some might argue that people are a lot like stuff. As we pile up our sin, all of our failures and misfires, we "lose value." In the eyes of others, or even in your own eyes, maybe you feel like your past makes you unworthy of love, undeserving of calling, and unqualified to succeed.

But if we are valued at the price someone would pay, then Jesus refutes all of those feelings by what He did for us at the cross. The cross of Jesus declares loudly, "You are not valued by the mess that you made but by the price that was paid."

Jesus not only paid the highest cost for you, deeming you valuable, but He is also a master restorer. Yesterday, we said that God is concerned with the full restoration of the entire world. If Jesus is God in flesh who came to reveal who God is in this world, then of course He would give us beautiful glimpses of restoration that will one day highlight the full restoration of the world.

To drive home this point, let's dive into some theology you may have learned from Owen Wilson in the movie *Meet the Parents.*

When Wilson's character, Kevin Rawley, was asked who inspired him to be a woodworker, Kevin said, "I guess I would have to say Jesus. JC was a carpenter, and I just figured if you're going to follow in someone's footsteps, who better than Christ?"[57]

For centuries, we've been taught that Joseph, Jesus's earthly father, was a carpenter—and that young Jesus would have watched His dad, learned from His dad, and eventually worked with His dad as a fellow carpenter. We learn this from Matthew 13:55, when the crowd in Jesus's hometown asks, **"Isn't this the carpenter's son?"** The Greek word *tekton* is translated as carpenter, but it has also been translated as "craftsman" or "builder," and it can be applied to working with both wood and stone.[58]

I have no doubt that Jesus would have been an excellent carpenter. In fact, I have no doubt that Jesus would be skilled at anything His hands were involved in. It may rock your world to see Jesus as a stonemason, but there is significant scholarship that would support this view. Hebraic scholar James W. Fleming surveyed northern Israel's landscape, and he noted that the majority of homes in Israel would have been constructed with stone and not wood. Therefore, he came to this conclusion: "Jesus and Joseph would have formed and made nine out of ten projects from stone either by chiseling or carving the stone or stacking building blocks."[59] Simply put, trying to make a living as a wood carpenter in a land where trees were scarce would have been extremely difficult.

Typically, when speakers or leaders are teaching, they will try to give a wide variety of references and analogies to help make the point come to life. Jesus was a master at this, often teaching through parables and illustrations. But I find it fascinating that there are so few references to wood or carpentry, not only from the mouth of Jesus, but in all of the Bible.

Instead, what we find are many references to stones, rocks, and buildings. Jesus, speaking of Himself in Matthew 21:42, said to the disciples, **"The stone the builders rejected has become the cornerstone."** Even our main character, Peter, was called "the rock." And as I mentioned earlier, this title was confirmed for him in front of a big rock formation at the foot of Mount Hermon.

Peter would then go on to describe the church this way in 1 Peter 2:4-5: **"As you come to him, the living Stone—rejected by humans but chosen by God and precious to him—you also, like living stones, are being built into a spiritual house to be a holy priesthood, offering spiritual sacrifices acceptable to God through Jesus Christ."**

Robby Galatty, writer and pastor, comments on these verses: "Notice that Peter refers to building a house with stones, an image that would have been quite familiar to those listening, and something Jesus may have been skilled in doing as a trained stonemason."[60]

In the church world, we often say the phrase, "God is in the restoration business." When we look deeper into it, we see that Jesus may have literally been in the restoration business with His father. How cool is that? But does this rethinking change anything? Not really. Whether Jesus worked with wood or stone doesn't change the fact that He saved the world and paid an astronomical price for you and me. However, seeing Jesus as a more well-rounded craftsman or builder helps you understand that no matter what materials God is presented with, He can not only restore its value, but in His hands, He can make it even more valuable.

He does it with material things. He also does it with His most prized possession, and that, my friend, is you. Jesus's death is a clear announcement that you are valuable to Him. All of us are like those long-lost treasures that show up on *Antiques Roadshow*. Except through Jesus we're so much more valuable, and we're no longer "long lost." We've been found—and by the grace of Jesus, we're now being filled with the Holy Spirit. Jesus is restoring and repurposing us for a purpose we cannot even imagine.

CHALLENGE

GOD NAMES YOU

Part of being restored is knowing who we are. The One who has naming rights over you is the One who created you! Open your Bible and read the following Bible verses. For each verse, record who God says you are. As a bonus, feel free to listen to the song "Who You Say I Am" by Hillsong in the background.

GENESIS 1:27	**ISAIAH 43:1**

JOHN 15:15	**ROMANS 8:17**

1 CORINTHIANS 3:9	**2 CORINTHIANS 5:17**

GALATIANS 2:20	EPHESIANS 2:10

EPHESIANS 2:19	COLOSSIANS 3:12

1 PETER 2:9	1 JOHN 3:1

Which one of these names means the most to you today, and why?

_____

_____

_____

28/40

DAY 29

ABANDON SHIP

People toss around a lot of words to describe Jesus, but very rarely have I seen the words "smart, brilliant, or intelligent." This is strange, considering all of the intricate details—the words, questions, and settings—that Jesus recreated in John 21. Jesus knew exactly what He was doing with every little, careful detail along the way.

Hear these words from Dallas Willard in his book *The Divine Conspiracy*.

> "At the literally mundane level Jesus knew how to transform the molecular structure of water to make it wine; that knowledge also allowed him to take a few pieces of bread and some little fish and feed thousands of people...He knew how to suspend gravity, interrupt weather patterns, eliminate unfruitful trees without saw or ax. He only needed a word. Surely, he must be amused at what Nobel prizes are awarded for today...Saying Jesus is Lord can mean little in practice for anyone who has to hesitate in saying Jesus is smart. He is not just nice, he is brilliant. He is the smartest man who has ever lived. He is now supervising the entire course of human history (Rev. 1:5) while simultaneously preparing the rest of the universe for our future role in it (John 14:2). He always has the best information on everything and certainly on the things that matter most in human life."[61]

We've already talked about how good Jesus was with His hands, but the best restorers also use their brains. They can look at a project from the start and know where it will one day end. They have the whole picture in mind before they start tinkering away. Even though they know the restoration project may require lots of work, with some unexpected ups and downs along the way, they can visualize something beautiful at the end. While Chip and Joanna Gaines may be the experts when it comes to fixing up and restoring homes, Jesus is the master expert and restorer of human lives. He knows how to perfectly chip away at us until He sees all of the gains in our life (cheesy, I know!).

Some might think Jesus to be a fool for still giving Peter the opportunity of a lifetime, even after all of the apostle's blunders. Maybe He would have fared better choosing someone else. But Jesus has the whole picture in mind. He knew fully well from the moment He called Peter that Peter would deny Him three times. But He also knew fully well who Peter would one day become. You can argue that the best restoration work of Peter happened in John 21, but this restoration project began years earlier, back in Luke 5.

On that day, the crowds were already starting to press in around Jesus. Without a proper amplification system to reach the crowds, the intelligent Jesus chose to use the natural acoustics of the water to amplify His message. Who needs a Bose system when you've got the Boat system? The text says there were only two boats on the water's edge that day, but Jesus chose to step into Peter's—a 50/50 chance, some might say. However, God doesn't operate with 50/50 odds. He knows exactly what He is doing. He is careful, brilliant, and specific in His rescue mission to save not just the world, but individuals like Peter along the way.

The Sea of Galilee, which forms the backdrop of so many stories in the life of Jesus, was an extremely important body of water because of the amount of fish that it provided. While there may have only been two boats at the water's edge in this specific instance, the Jewish historian Josephus tells us that at the time over 230 fishing boats were working on the Sea of Galilee.[62]

When Jesus chose the boat to preach from, it wasn't a case of Jesus saying, "Eeny, meeny, miny, moe," and by chance landing on Peter's boat. This wasn't 50/50.

This was 1 out of 230—less than ½ of a 1-percent chance. In other words, it was no accident that He stepped into Peter's boat. Jesus carefully chose Peter to be His rock, even knowing that it would take Peter many long, topsy-turvy years to live up to that name. He chose Peter to change the world, even though the fisherman didn't hold a position of power and prestige.

Jesus selects who man rejects.

So Jesus stepped into Peter's boat. So what?

I hope that you see this was not a random chance, but rather, the grace of Jesus in Peter's life. God had already been writing a beautiful story for Peter before the apostle had even met the author of his life.

Fishing is a noble profession, practical and worthwhile, especially for the community in which Peter lived. But God, the ultimate restorer, looks past externals, such as our profession, and sees what's going on inside of each one of us. He steps into each of our lives—each of our "boats," you might say—and He brings restoration and relief.

While we may not know all of the details of Peter's life leading up to this moment, we know that being "unschooled," as Acts 4:13 describes him, might mean that he didn't have what it takes to follow a rabbi. If that were the case, Jesus would've known if Peter was floundering in life, even sinking. But Jesus wasn't going to let him slowly sink in life any more than when Peter was literally sinking while walking on water. Jesus offered him a better alternative. He offered him an opportunity of greater significance and purpose. He was calling Peter to abandon ship and follow Him.

I don't know what "boat" your life has put you in right now. You might be on a boat that provides you a stable income and is worthwhile to society. You might be on a boat that is helping no one and quickly sinking. But no matter what boat you are in, God knows your heart. He knows if you are sinking.

Sadly, many of us are. Even many of those who profess to be Christians are still searching for purpose. Too many of us are waffling in life, not living with true meaning, purpose, and fulfillment, even though Jesus offers a life to the fullest.

Purpose is ultimately found in following Jesus. Fulfillment is found in turning your life over to Him. Some of us never get to experience "great" because we never leave good enough behind. Jesus said so in Mark 8:36, **"What good is it for someone to gain the whole world, yet forfeit their soul?"**

Just as Jesus stepped into Peter's boat, He steps into your boat today. He knows your story. He knows you won't live a perfect life. But He also knows fully well who you will become one day, even if you don't know yet!

The invitation is the same for you as it was for Peter: **"Follow me."**

God doesn't ask everyone to stop fishing—to cast aside your profession. All of us have a job and a calling, and for some, God's call is to stay in what we're doing. Levi Lusko says, "Sometimes in following after God, there is more faith in staying than there is in going."[63] Many on the water that day would leave their jobs to become followers of Jesus. For most of the others in the 228 boats, Jesus didn't call them to abandon ship, but to stay, to fish, and to be His followers in the midst of their families and communities.

Meaning and significance are found less in our occupation than in our obedience to step into the call to follow Jesus. If it feels like you are sinking, why not put your life into the hands of the ultimate Restorer and your story into the brilliant mind of the Author?

CHALLENGE

NAME YOUR CHAPTERS

Read Psalm 139:13-16. These words tell us how God beautifully crafted each of us as human beings, and He wrote our stories before we even existed. As you read these verses, record your thoughts and feelings in the margin.

> **"For you created my inmost being;**
> **you knit me together in my mother's womb.**
> **I praise you because I am fearfully and wonderfully made;**
> **your works are wonderful,**
> **I know that full well.**
> **My frame was not hidden from you**
> **when I was made in the secret place,**
> **when I was woven together in the depths of the earth.**
> **Your eyes saw my unformed body;**
> **all the days ordained for me were written in your book**
> **before one of them came to be."**

God is writing a story through you. Today, your challenge is to think about your life as a story. On the front cover of the book on the facing page, insert your full name as the title and feel free to draw or add a subtitle. In the Table of Contents, we've included ten spaces for chapter titles. I've taken the liberty to write down the names for chapter 1 and 10. Write the names of chapters 2 to 6 today. However, leave chapters 7 to 9 blank because we will come to those later in the book.

-GOD

TABLE OF CONTENTS

1. FEARFULLY & WONDERFULLY CREATED
2. _____
3. _____
4. _____
5. _____

6. _____
7. _____
8. _____
9. _____
10. FOREVER FREE WITH KING JESUS

29/40

DAY 30

FORGIVENESS MOVES FORWARD

Forgiveness is a two-fold process.

1 **TO CANCEL THE DEBT**

2 **TO STOP FEELING ANGER OR RESENTMENT TOWARD SOMEONE**

During the week of absolution, we spent time describing the first part of the process—namely, how Jesus has canceled the debt of our sins. His death on the cross paid in full the bill for all mankind. This means that Peter, and you, and me, and your spouse, and your dad, and your neighbor, are all included.

To cancel a debt is one thing. It is the second part of the forgiving process that many of us fail to receive in full, hindering us from experiencing the freedom God wants for us.

The first piece of forgiveness was settled with an action. The second focuses on an attitude.

It's one thing to have a bill paid when we didn't deserve it. It's another thing for the person who paid that bill to still love you, show up for you, care for you, and want the best for you. This is the piece of forgiveness that takes longer for most of us to wrap our minds around.

If someone pays a bill for you, but remains angry with you, then you are not free. If someone still hangs that bill over your head, or constantly brings up either your sin or how much they had to pay for your sin, how is that freedom? Or if someone paid your bill in full, but then required you to somehow, directly or indirectly, pay it off with interest over time, that's not true forgiveness; that's a business loan.

True forgiveness loves with both action and attitude.

But how can you tell if you are not angry or resentful, either toward someone else or toward yourself? Here's an easy test…

Do you continue to point backward or do you strive to move forward? Anger and resentment always point backward, whereas true forgiveness strives forward.

A lot of people think God is angry with them. But if God is still angry with you, then why would He desire to move you forward?"

Anger looks backward and says, "I forget you." God looks forward and says, "I forgive you."

In the story of Peter, we have already noted how Jesus took the first step by arriving on the shore that day and recreating the first and the worst moments of their relationship. Some might think that recreating past moments is a sign that Jesus is angry with him. Maybe He's being cruel to Peter, seeking to publicly shame him. But that would go against everything the Bible teaches and the overall rescue mission of Jesus. Remember, John 3:17 says, **"For God did not send His Son into world to condemn the world, but to save the world through Him."**

Let's enter back into the fireside chat again from the 89th Chapter to see a beautiful truth come to life:

> **"When they had finished eating, Jesus said to Simon Peter, 'Simon son of John, do you love me more than these?'**
>> **"'Yes, Lord,' he said, 'you know that I love you.'**
>> **"Jesus said, 'Feed my lambs.'**
>> **"Again Jesus said, 'Simon son of John, do you love me?'**
>> **"He answered, 'Yes, Lord, you know that I love you.'**
>> **"Jesus said, 'Take care of my sheep.'**
>> **"The third time he said to him, 'Simon son of John, do you love me?'**
>> **"Peter was hurt because Jesus asked him the third time, 'Do you love me?' He said, 'Lord, you know all things; you know that I love you.'**
>> **"Jesus said, 'Feed my sheep.'"**

Jesus isn't interested in making Peter feel worse or experience more shame. How do we know this? If Jesus were angry with Peter, resented Peter, or wanted to shame Peter, in which direction would Jesus point? Backward. But in what direction does Jesus point? Forward.

While Peter is still pining about his failure, Jesus is busy painting his future.

Even when Peter changes the word "love" to what many believe is a lesser kind of love (see Day 23), it doesn't rattle Jesus. He still points Peter forward.

> **"Feed my lambs. Take care of my sheep. Feed my sheep."**

ANGER LOOKS
BACKWARD AND
SAYS, "I FORGET YOU."
GOD LOOKS FORWARD
AND SAYS,
"I FORGIVE YOU."

#FORGIVINGCHALLENGE

This is a clarion call for Peter to lead and step back into the calling of being the pastor of the very first church. This was the call that Jesus first gave to Peter based on his confession in Matthew 16:13-19 (see Day 7). One of the analogies most commonly associated with pastors is that of shepherds. By saying, "Feed my sheep," Jesus declared to Peter that He still needed him to be the pastor of the first church.

This is a very clear call from Jesus to not only receive the declaration of forgiveness, given on the cross; it's also an invitation to move forward into the call that Jesus had previously placed on his life. The absolution given by Jesus on the cross was the outside action needed to save Peter for eternity, but what truly shows the heart and attitude of Jesus is His invitation to move Peter forward.

When we describe the opposite of freedom, we often use words or analogies like prisons, chains, slavery, walls, and debts. All of these are obstacles meant to hold us back. When we harbor anger toward ourselves or someone else, we are intentionally or unintentionally putting up a wall, shackling both ourselves and the other person, or holding on to the debt.

By the charcoal fire, God removes those obstacles from Peter so that he could freely move forward in the life and calling that He had originally invited him into.

This is not the action of an angry God, but a loving God.

Mike Foster writes, "Jesus wipes away tears of regret and hands out grace-filled snow cones on hot judgmental days. Jesus is for us, and He really wants to help."[64]

Jesus didn't recreate the fire to bring charges upon Peter from the past but rather to charge him to move forward.

CHALLENGE

BACKWARD OR FORWARD?

Answer and elaborate on the five questions below:

1 Do you tend to move forward or backward in life?

_____

_____

2 Are you still angry with yourself about something?

_____

_____

3 Are you still resentful toward yourself about anything?

_____

_____

4 Is there something in your past that keeps you from moving forward?

_____

_____

5 Has God charged you with a clear call in your life that you have been avoiding?

_____

_____

30/40

DAY 31

MORE THAN THESE?

Jesus is the master of questions. In the book, *Jesus is the Question*, Martin Copenhaver tells us that Jesus asks a total of 307 questions in the Gospels. Meanwhile, Jesus is asked 183 questions, but He only directly answered three. In other words, for every question He answers directly, He asks a hundred![65]

One of Jesus's most important questions was directed at Peter. After finishing breakfast, Jesus starts the charcoal-fire conversation by asking him: **"Simon son of John, do you love me more than these?"**

Uh-oh. Jesus just said Peter's full name. When full names get thrown around, you know serious business is about to come. I dreaded the three words, "Zachary Andrew Zehnder," especially in my middle school years, because I knew I was about to get punished. Now, as a parent, using the full name of my children is a nice wild card to hold. If all else fails, I can automatically escalate the situation by saying their full legal name, and they will know it's time to pay attention. Dad is serious.

While saying someone's full name almost always equals serious business, there have been a few occasions when my full name is used, not because of something bad that I had done, but to mark a special occasion in my life.

- On my baptism day: "Zachary Andrew Zehnder, I baptize you in the name of the Father, the Son, and the Holy Spirit."

- On my wedding day: "I, Zachary Andrew Zehnder, take you, Allison Emi Buck, to be my wife, to have and to hold, from this day forward, for better, for worse, for richer, for poorer, in sickness and in health, until death do us part." Best decision I ever made by the way!

- On my graduation day: My diploma displayed my full name.

- On the day I became a homeowner: I signed my full legal name. I was not used to doing this, so I had to practice my cursive to ensure that I could write my middle name legibly.

- On my ordination into ministry: As hands were placed on me to become a pastor, my full name was spoken.

Jesus uses Peter's full name at the charcoal fire not to threaten him, but to mark it as a special occasion. But in analyzing this first question of Jesus—"Do you love me more than these?"—scholars debate who or what Jesus is talking about with the word "these."

Some scholars believe "these" could have been Jesus pointing at the fish, the nets, or the boats. A few verses earlier, Peter hauls in 153 fish all by himself, even though Jesus has already prepared breakfast. The fish are probably right there next to them. This answer would make sense. After failing Jesus, Peter goes back to fishing, a fine profession, but not the one into which Jesus had called him. So maybe Jesus points at the fish and asks, "Do you love me more than these?" This would be a subtle way of saying to Peter, "Are you sure you want to go back to fishing when I have called you to something more?"

Other scholars believe the "these" Jesus is referencing are not the fish, but the other disciples who were also enjoying the breakfast. It was around a different meal, the Last Supper, where Peter's public unraveling truly began. On that night, Jesus predicted not only that He would die, but that all of His disciples would fall away in the midst of this tragic turn of events. In response, Mark 14:29-31 says:

"Peter declared, 'Even if all fall away, I will not.'

"'Truly I tell you,' Jesus answered, 'today—yes, tonight—before the rooster crows twice you yourself will disown me three times.'

"But Peter insisted emphatically, 'Even if I have to die with you, I will never disown you.'"

Rather than simply saying, "I will never fall away from you, Jesus," Peter takes it a step further by disparaging all of the other disciples. "Even if all of THEM fall away, I will not." The other disciples were present to see this exchange, and they certainly knew that what Jesus had predicted had come to fruition. We've seen already that Peter had much sorrow over his denials of Jesus, but I'm sure he also was humiliated and contrite with his friends. He shouldn't have said that they were far more likely to disown Jesus.

So which is it: Are the "these" the fish or the disciples? Why can't it be both? After all, Jesus is brilliant (see Day 29), so He could have included both in this single statement. But I would argue there's a bigger thing happening here. Have you ever wondered why Jesus would ask Peter this question in front of the other disciples?

Some would argue that by doing this publicly, Jesus would have brought more shame to Peter. Maybe Jesus is just "making an example" out of Peter to the other disciples. But that's not the case.

DO YOU LOVE JESUS MORE THAN ANYTHING?

#FORGIVINGCHALLENGE

For Peter to accomplish the mission that Jesus entrusted to him, Peter would need the full support of the disciples behind him. The only way to ensure that Peter would get their support was for them to hear from Jesus that Peter was forgiven and fully restored. Jesus marked this occasion, using Peter's full name, in front of the other disciples, to show them that Peter "is still my guy."

Without this moment, it's possible that the disciples would have still held ill-will toward Peter. Rev. Jerry Watts says, "A discerning reading of the post crucifixion gospels reveals that the gospel writers probably had given up on Peter as he is only mentioned marginally until John 21. Isn't that like us, when someone falls we tend to toss them under the bus?"[66]

It would take the public endorsement of Jesus for the other disciples to fully throw their weight and support behind Peter in the future, especially after Peter claimed he would never fall away like the others would. Not only did Jesus meet Peter by the fire that day to restore him, but He also recreated this moment to soften the hearts of the disciples toward His leading man.

While we may have doubts about the meaning of this question—"Do you love me more than these?"—Jesus used this question, as well as the conversation that followed, to mark a special occasion. And this special occasion would erase any doubts about Peter's future and the future of the church.

IDENTIFY YOUR 'THESE'

What if Jesus asked you the same thing today: "Do you love me more than these?" How would you respond?

_____

_____

What are your "these"? What is prone to get in the way of truly following Jesus wherever He calls? Keep in mind that your "these" don't have to be bad things. Even good things can at times get in the way of following Jesus.

_____

_____

Describe as best you can what it would look like to be faithfully following after God? What would you do? Who would you be with? Where would you go?

_____

_____

Your challenge is to take one step in this direction today. What step did you take?

_____

_____

31/40

DAY 32

THE COMFORTING COMMANDER

Jesus made four predictions at the Last Supper:

1. HE WOULD DIE AND RISE FROM THE DEAD THREE DAYS LATER.

2. JUDAS ISCARIOT WOULD BETRAY HIM.

3. PETER WOULD DENY HIM THREE TIMES.

4. ALL HIS DISCIPLES WOULD FALL AWAY ON ACCOUNT OF HIM.

Many sermons and stories have been told of the first three predictions, but not many are written about the fourth.

On the night and morning before the crucifixion of Jesus, we witness a disastrous performance from the twelve disciples. Judas Iscariot sold and betrayed Jesus for thirty shekels of silver, which would likely be worth something in the neighborhood of a few hundred dollars today. Only two disciples, John and Peter, could bear to watch Jesus being tortured. Peter watched Jesus being taunted, but he did so from a distance, on the outskirts of the courtyard by the charcoal fire. He first denied Jesus in front of a single servant girl, but by the end of these encounters, he was even offering up curses. John remained near Jesus, and to his credit, consoled the Lord's mother during the crucifixion. But nowhere does it say that John spoke up or stood up for Jesus in that moment. When Jesus most needed a friend, His trusted twelve crumbled like a house of cards in a hurricane.

It wasn't just Peter who was sorrowful over his behavior. The Bible later says that Judas Iscariot was filled with so much grief over his sin that he would commit suicide. This, by the way, is where the devil wants you to eventually take all of your grief. He wants you to hold on to it until it kills you. The disciples were a mixed bag of emotions. Not only were they grieving the death of Jesus, but I'm sure they were confused and sad over their one-time friend, Judas, taking his life. On top of all of that, they were embarrassed and disappointed by their own actions. They were fearful of the political leaders coming after them. And perhaps because of the sudden death of Jesus, they were led to doubt all that had happened over the past few years.

Things weren't the same.

While we have been largely focusing on the freedom that Jesus brings to Peter, I don't want to gloss over the fact that Jesus shows up repeatedly to all of the disciples. In addition, while much of the New Testament centers around these twelve men, Jesus had many other devoted followers.

Take a look at John 20. In the chapter prior to Peter's restoration, Jesus reaches out to several integral friends and followers to restore them. He comes to them, even though many of them had failed Him in His hardest, darkest moment. He comes to them as they are going through a whirlwind of emotions, experiencing tears, fears, and doubts. (I'm borrowing those terms from N.T. Wright's book *God and the Pandemic*, a short, little book and a fabulous read.)[67]

First, you have Mary Magdalene crying at the empty tomb. Isn't it amazing that the first person whom Jesus shows up to after the resurrection is a woman? To include a woman in such an integral fashion would defy the ideals and norms of the culture in that day. This revolutionary, counter-cultural concept is a clear announcement that there are no limits to who can follow Jesus. Come one, come all, come men, come women, come old, come young. Diving deeper into this, it's pretty obvious in the crucifixion accounts that the women disciples (almost all of them named Mary for some reason) were even more faithful than the men. This is how I know the Bible isn't made up. If it were a concocted story, the author(s) wouldn't give so many characters the same name! It's confusing!

As Mary Magdalene is crying, Jesus shows up in her tears, and says in John 20:15, **"Woman, why are you crying?"** After comforting her, He then calls her to go and tell the disciples that He is alive.

Later that night, the disciples are quarantined in a room out of fear. These same disciples, who were runaways on the night before Jesus's death, are now huddled together in one room. A crowd of cowards. Suddenly, Jesus bursts through the wall, and His first statement, found in Luke 24:36, is **"Peace be with you."** He doesn't mock them, scold them, or hold what they did against them. He's just doing what Jesus has always done: announcing that the peace of God is still available. After showing them His scars, He sent them to go and tell others the Good News. But He didn't leave them empty-handed. Just a couple of chapters later, in the book of Acts, He would fill them with the Holy Spirit.

Finally, a full week later, but in the same room with the doors still locked, Jesus bursts through the wall again, making a special appearance to the one disciple who wasn't there a week earlier. His name, if you remember in our introduction, was Thomas, most commonly referred to as "Doubting Thomas." Jesus said to him, "Stop doubting and believe." He then revealed his nail-scarred hands to Thomas, who then believed. After Jesus spoke a blessing over his life, Thomas would turn from doubting to devoted (John 20:24-29).

JESUS DIDN'T JUST
FREE YOU FROM THE
CONSEQUENCES
OF SIN; HE FREED
YOU TO LIVE A LIFE
OF MEANING AND
PURPOSE.

#FORGIVINGCHALLENGE

God knows who you are. He knows what you need. While the death and resurrection of Jesus assures our eternity, God actually wants you to know that right here, right now, there is a purpose for you. Jesus didn't just free you from the consequences of sin; He freed you to live a life of meaning and purpose. As you go about this new life, no matter if tears, fears, doubts, or any other wave of emotions crashes over you, Jesus shows up.

"Why are you crying? Peace be with you. Stop doubting and believe."

Jesus led with comforting words, but in each case He would issue a command. He canceled your debt. Let that comfort you. But His work as a restorer will never be done until we see Jesus face-to-face. Until then, He will never stop pursuing you. Jesus will never get tired of visiting you. He will always give you just what you need—and He will send you out again with a command and a call to be His representation in this world.

CHALLENGE

TEARS, FEARS, AND DOUBTS

Write any tears, fears, or doubts you may be experiencing when it comes to walking in faith with Jesus:

TEARS

_____

_____

_____

FEARS

_____

_____

_____

DOUBTS

_____

_____

_____

After writing down your tears, fears, or doubts, see and say the words of Jesus to yourself over each thing you recorded.

"Why are you crying? Peace be with you. Stop doubting and believe."

32/40

DAY 33

FULLY RESTORED

Paul closes his second letter to the Corinthian church with this command: **"Strive for full restoration." 2 Corinthians 13:11**

What does full restoration look like?

One of the most complete pictures of full restoration is in #Chapter89. So far in our story, Jesus has already restored Peter back to the integral position of leading the early church. But He's about to go even further to fully restore Peter to not only be the person that God wants him to be, but also the person that Peter wants to become.

Check out Jesus's next words following the three questions—a part of the story that is often overlooked. John 21:18-19 says:

> **"'Very truly I tell you, when you were younger you dressed yourself and went where you wanted; but when you are old you will stretch out your hands, and someone else will dress you and lead you where you do not want to go.' Jesus said this to indicate the kind of death by which Peter would glorify God. Then he said to him, 'Follow me!'**

It has been all good news to this point. But now Jesus says that following Him would ultimately cost Peter his life. Uh-oh.

Contrary to what some teach and, sadly, many believe, there is a significant cost to following Jesus. We live in a world that tries to avoid any form of suffering at all costs, but this is not possible for a follower of Jesus. Jesus reminded His followers that times of suffering would come their way. Here, Jesus *assures* Peter that this high call on his life will ultimately be met with a high price.

But there is something deeply beautiful about this call given to Peter. Jesus has already given Peter a second chance at leading the early church. Now He's giving Peter a chance to become the man that Peter has always wanted to be. While Peter may be best known for his three denials, remember that it was ultimately Peter's brash claim around the supper table that started him on this downward spiral.

> **"But Peter declared, 'Even if I have to die with you, I will never disown you.'" Matthew 26:35a**

What Peter wanted most was to be a faithful disciple of Jesus—a loyal, committed friend whom Jesus could always count on, no matter what. Instead of a faithful follower, however, the first charcoal fire only proved he was a fickle, flawed, and fragile follower.

At the end of it all, Peter wanted to live up to the name that Jesus had placed on him—"the rock." At the end of it all, I believe that's what all of us who follow Jesus want. We want to live up to the name that Jesus gives to us.

The truth is that God has been good to us in all of our stories. His grace made a way in our lives when we had nothing left to give on our own. He demonstrated His love for us not when we had our lives fully together, but while we were still sinners. In response to how good God has been to us, we want nothing more than to live a holy life that makes Him proud. We choose to follow Jesus not because we *have* to, but because we *want* to. We want to live a life of gratitude toward God. And when we fail, especially after how much God has done for us, we feel terrible. We want to do better.

This call to Peter assures us that God wants to fully restore all of us. He wants to help us become the people that we ourselves, after receiving God's grace, want to become. The cross and tomb saved Peter's eternal life, while the second charcoal fire saved Peter's earthly life. Jesus gave meaning and purpose to a man who was uncertain whether he should just go back to fishing. When we mess up, we spend a lot of time wondering if we are still able to walk in the calling that Jesus places on our lives. The answer is that Jesus's grace makes us worthy to do so.

His call is deeper than just "believe in me so that you are saved when you die." His call is that right here, right now, you can follow me. The perennial call that Jesus offers to His disciples more than any other call is found in two words, **"Follow me."**

Unfortunately, many Christians treat following Jesus as if it is a burden to bear. Jesus says there will be great cost to follow Him. But the cost of not fully following Jesus is far greater.

Walking *without* Jesus leads to a lack of direction, confusion, purposelessness, and unfulfilled lives.

Walking *with* Jesus leads to meaning, purpose, joy, and fulfillment.

Some may look at the prediction of Peter's death as a bad ending, but this was the single best ending Peter could have ever asked for. To walk fully with Jesus all the way until the end. To become the "big boulder" that Jesus always knew he would become. Ironically, it was an impending death sentence hanging over Peter's life

JESUS SAYS THERE WILL BE GREAT COST TO FOLLOW HIM. BUT THE COST OF NOT FULLY FOLLOWING JESUS IS FAR GREATER.

#FORGIVINGCHALLENGE

that would bring him the freedom he so desperately needed. Death is never the final chapter in stories that God writes because resurrection always comes next. Peter's hope in eternal life, which he knew would be waiting for him on the other side, allowed him to fully embrace a death sentence in this world. With God, even death sentences can become freedom announcements.

We don't have to wait to walk in freedom until we see Jesus in heaven. We can walk in freedom today, right here, right now. There is nothing that you could have ever done, or will do that our God cannot restore. Nothing. God is good with His hands. Whether His hands are busy creating the world, working as a stonemason, or being nailed to a cross, God never stops creating masterpieces.

You are a masterpiece. Ephesians 2:10 (NLT) says, **"For we are God's masterpiece. He has created us anew in Christ Jesus, so we can do the good things he planned for us long ago."**

God has fearfully and wonderfully made you. He's put a high calling on your life and prepared a beautiful journey for you. Believe in Jesus for your eternity, but also believe in Jesus for your NOW by walking in the calling He places on your life. Become the masterpiece that you know you want to become. Be free.

CHALLENGE

"YOU" VERSION 2.0

Memorize Ephesians 2:10 (NLT): **"For we are God's masterpiece. He has created us anew in Christ Jesus, so we can do the good things he planned for us long ago."** Start by writing it down three times in the space below.

_____

_____

_____

_____

_____

_____

Do you believe that you are a masterpiece? Why or why not?

_____

_____

Describe in detail what a fully restored version of you would look like.

_____

_____

33/40

DAYS
34-40

OF THE   40-DAY

CHALLENGE

S.C.A.R.S.

SANCTIF

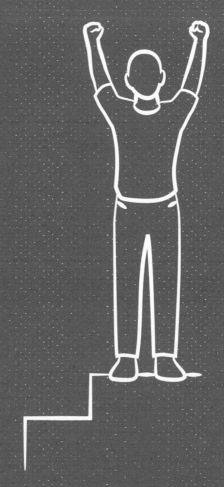

ICATION

DAY 34

FREEDOM MOUNTAIN

You have made it a long way on this journey, but you have one final important step to take to truly be free. To get to the top of Freedom Mountain requires many steps, some more difficult than others. However, before we reach the mountaintop experience of freedom together, let's review where we've been so far.

SIN

It is difficult to get to the top of Freedom Mountain. You spent a lot of time training for this climb and now you're mustering up as much strength as you can to begin. However, you are shocked as you struggle to take even a single, solitary step in the right direction. As you try to navigate your way to the top, you stumble and fall. You keep veering down paths you were never intended to follow. Your errors begin multiplying, and now an already difficult climb is becoming impossible. Every error adds heavy baggage to the climb, and you are exhausted. For some reason, even if you can't rationalize it, you feel the need to keep holding on to the baggage. Now, it takes everything inside of you to attempt a single step. Eventually, you crash. The climb is over. You've failed.

CONFESSION

You admit that there is no way to get to the top on your own. You confess that the mountain is too big, and you are too weak. Your journey is over. A deep sadness comes over you. But in your sorrow, another man suddenly comes down the mountain and finds you lying there. He's got some exciting news to share with you.

He asks you to follow Him. He lifts you up, leads you around a bend, and shows you a new path.

There's something unique about this man, even if you can't explain it. He claims this path will lead all the way to the top. But as you examine the path, it doesn't appear all that impressive. It certainly doesn't look appealing. It's rather narrow. Nobody would choose this path on their own. You wouldn't even know how to find it if it hadn't been shown to you. You remind Him that even if the pathway leads to the top, you can't get there. Your bags weigh far too much. You do your best to describe what is in each and every bag. But you've forgotten what is in some bags, while you remember only small details about other bags. As sorrow comes over you, the man shows great kindness. Nothing about the bags that you are describing seems to faze this man.

ABSOLUTION

The man then offers to carry your bags for you. To be sure, you can use the break. They have been weighing you down, and you are ready to release them. As He reaches for your first bag, you notice a nasty scar in the middle of His hand. He picks up your first bag, then your second, your third. You lose count, and honestly you didn't even realize how many bags you were carrying. Pretty soon, He has picked them all up. At first you were impressed by this man's kindness, but now you're staggered by His amazing strength. You would have never guessed by looking at Him that He could be so strong. The bags felt like bricks to you, but He throws them over His shoulders like bags of feathers. How is this possible? Surely this man will eventually tire, but it certainly doesn't look like it anytime soon.

RESTORATION

This man walks with strength, and there's a joy in His steps. He never once complains about the weight of your bags or makes you feel guilty about having to carry them. Instead, He talks on and on about how excited He is for you to join Him at the top. He assures you it's a view that you've never seen before. When you get thirsty, He asks for your empty water bottle, taps on a rock, and somehow water flows from the stone, filling the bottle. What in the world!? As you drink, this fresh water tastes like no other water you've ever had before! Somehow, even though you just chugged a full bottle, not a drop is gone. It's still filled to the brim. This makes no sense.

There's only a short distance left until you get to the top. The last steps are difficult, so you'll need some nourishment to sustain you. The man starts a fire and begins cooking over this open flame. Soon, you're eating the best fish you've ever had in your life. But where in the world did He get this fish? After eating, He calls you to follow Him again. With every step up the mountain, He is more and more giddy. He's so excited you are with Him.

SANCTIFICATION

You are almost to the top. The man runs ahead to ensure that everything is in order for you when you reach the peak. But just as He leaves, you notice how steep and dangerous this last step truly is. If you don't land the step well, it would have severe consequences. Because of the high grade, you can't fully see what's on the other side of the mountain. Doubt and fear begin to creep in. You wonder if the view is even worth it. You're reminded that the path He led you on didn't look that impressive. Maybe this view won't be impressive either. Besides, you have made it up pretty far and can see some cool things where you are. Taking this final step would require great courage. Do you really have what it takes? In the midst of your doubts and fears, He shows up again. He can sense your nervousness, so He offers to take the step with you. He reaches His other hand out to you, and you see a similar scar on this hand as well. He invites you to take this nail-scarred hand and take the final step with Him.

Will you take the last step?

I hope you would say, "Yes!"

And yet, can you believe it, this is the step that keeps so many from total freedom.

In the above illustration, as in life, there are several exit points that you can take on your journey to be free. The earliest exit point is when you commit a sin. If you refuse to bring your sin to God, you will never be free. The next exit point is refusing to believe God paid the price for your sin. Another exit point is refusing to believe that God fully restores you. At any point, any of these refusals will only lead to more bondage.

The final exit point, however, is the saddest for me. It's where I see so many leave the journey. What a tragedy that one can be so close to freedom, and yet they don't experience it because they were one step short. Jesus didn't do all that He did for you so that you stop short anywhere. Jesus stepped down so that you would step up with Him.

True freedom doesn't happen until you step up into the freedom God has won for you and wants for you. This process of stepping into freedom is called sanctification.

As we mentioned on Day 5, the definition of sanctification is the process of being freed from sin. Other definitions of sanctification are to be holy, or set apart, but the ultimate purpose is to be free. It's when we live a holy and set-apart life that we are truly free.

With sanctification, we participate in this process with God's Holy Spirit inside of us. We cooperate with God in sanctification. However, the devil knows that the best place to attack us on our journey to freedom are the places where you and I are the most involved. He will throw everything that He can against us in this last and final step. This, by the way, is why so many leave the journey of freedom here.

In fact, Satan will make this last step seem impossible. But remember the Good News. God has called you to ascend to the mountaintop, and you can rest assured that He's given you everything you need to make it all the way up. The God who was with you after you fell taking the first step is still with you as you take the last step. Come, and ascend to the top of Freedom Mountain.

My question to you again is: "Will you take the last step?"

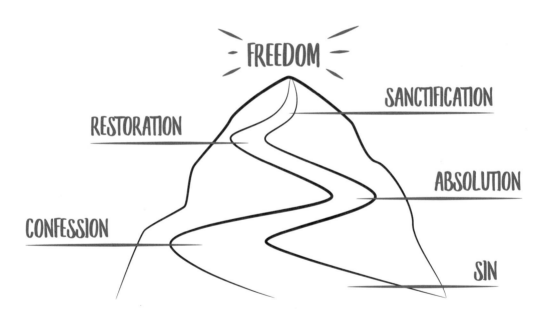

CHALLENGE

MOUNTAIN STEPPING

Identify the phase of Freedom Mountain that is the hardest for you to climb or get past. This could be where your journey to freedom has stopped in the past.

Write down why this is the most difficult phase for you to climb. What leads you to exit your journey to freedom here? What can you do in the future to climb past this phase?

_____

_____

_____

_____

_____

_____

_____

_____

_____

_____

_____

34/40

DAY 35

THE TATTOO PREACHER GUY

How does a preacher with no tattoos on his body get to be known as "The Tattoo Preacher Guy?" I'll tell you!

If you preach for a living, you are bound to say something you didn't mean. Most of the time, these slip-ups have no consequences and you can laugh at them later. One time, though, my unintentional words from a message in March of 2014 went viral and made international headlines.

I was in the middle of a 22-week series on the book of 1 Corinthians. As I was preaching on 1 Corinthians 8, a chapter focused on meat sacrificed to idols, I noted that I'd never had a single pastoral counseling session on this topic. This, however, was a divisive issue for the Corinthian church. Some said you could never eat meat sacrificed to idols, while others maintained that in their Christian liberty, they were free to eat this meat at any time. Rather than choosing a side, Paul's main concern was less on whether it was okay to eat the meat or not, but rather on what kind of witness they would be if they partook of this practice.

In the church today, there are many divisive issues among well-meaning Christians with polar-opposite views. One of those issues is tattoos. In the middle of this particular message, I sarcastically said that I would pay for anyone who wanted to get a tattoo of our church logo. I told them that it would be really good marketing for our church. I was joking, of course, and went on to finish the message.

After the worship service, someone came up to me and said, "I want to take you up on your offer for the free tattoo. This church has meant a lot to me and my story, and I'd be honored to wear that logo." I said, "Wait, are you serious?" I then asked him to give me a day to think and pray through this.

During those twenty-four hours, I sought godly counsel from friends, searched the Bible, and read through many commentaries. At the end of it all, I felt very similar to the way Paul felt when he was writing to the Corinthians. My conclusion was that whether or not someone has a tattoo, what's most important is the kind of witness this person would be to the world.

At the end of the day, I decided to fulfill my end of the deal. After all of the dust had settled, twenty-three people got a tattoo of our church logo on their bodies. The story went viral and was found on the top news sites like Yahoo, Huffington Post, and Fox News.

I learned a lot about the tattoo world. I never realized until that moment how controversial the topic of tattoos is among Christians today. Most tattoos have special meaning or a deeper story attached to them—and the men and women who have tattoos, generally, love to talk about them.

Our church logo has a cross at its center. All of the men and women who ended up with our logo tattooed on their body would have a story to tell, not just about our church, but more importantly, about Jesus. This particular mark would give them the opportunity to tell of the remarkable victory Jesus won for all of us at the cross. These men and women would forever have an opportunity to tell the story of Jesus to people whom I likely never would be able to reach.

Two days after our story aired on the local news station, a woman came to our church—a woman who had many tattoos. She hadn't been to church in over ten years. Her prior perception of the church was that it was judgmental, hypocritical, and unfriendly. Two members from the church had been asking her to come for over a year but nothing happened. After seeing the story of our church, she finally made her way through our doors. After the worship gathering, she sent me a message about how welcoming the church was and how excited she was to walk with us in the future.

This was one of hundreds of stories and messages that I received from people all across the world. I remember a young adult from Atlanta who messaged me about how ostracized she was from her church after she got a tattoo of a butterfly in memory of her grandmother. The sad reality is that she really did miss being a part of the church and longed for a church like ours where she and all of her tattoos could be welcome. She wanted to follow Jesus but couldn't find a church that would welcome her.

Just as outer marks like tattoos tell a story, so too, we tell a story with our lives.

A couple of decades after the conversation around the second charcoal fire, Peter would go on to write words that still encourage us today. 1 Peter 2:11-12 says: **"Dear friends, I urge you, as foreigners and exiles, to abstain from sinful desires, which wage war against your soul. Live such good lives among the pagans that, though they accuse you of doing wrong, they may see your good deeds and glorify God on the day he visits us."**

In the first verse of this passage, Peter reminds us how important it is to flee from sin, which is always lurking, always waging war. Peter knows from firsthand experience what it means to lose this war. He knows that when we lose this battle, we are left with feelings of guilt, shame, and regret.

THE GREATEST MARK
YOU CAN LEAVE IN THIS
WORLD IS TO USE YOUR
FORGIVEN, REDEEMED,
AND RESTORED LIFE TO
HELP SOMEONE ELSE
EXPERIENCE THE FREEDOM
GOD HAS FOR THEM.

#FORGIVINGCHALLENGE

Instead of going further down a path that leads to destruction, Peter invites us into a life of good works. It is possible, he says, for others to see the good works in us and glorify God. He reminds us that what we do with our lives does, in fact, matter. When we work in tandem, step-by-step, with God, we are capable of helping others come to an eternal relationship with Him.

After we missed the mark through something in our past, our stories could have ended there. But, amazingly, God gives us infinite chances to write new chapters, new endings. Those of us who have been freed from our sin can now use our lives to bring glory to God.

If we never step into the freedom that God has for us, or the good works He has prepared for us, then we will always fall short of what we could have been.

Most people talk about wanting to leave a mark in this world. But many stories end with the person missing the mark. They have done or said something that they can never get past. They never reach their full potential.

The reality is that "we cannot un-see what we've seen or un-live what we've lived. We can, however—with the strength of the One who conquers death—move forward," says Mike Foster in *Freeway*.[68]

Other people, after having been marked by God's grace and equipped with His power, will forever leave a mark. The greatest mark you can leave in this world is to use your forgiven, redeemed, and restored life to help someone else experience the freedom God has for them.

Will your story's final chapter be about missing the mark or leaving a mark that brings freedom to others?

CHALLENGE

NAME YOUR MARK

What mark do you want to leave in this world? On Day 7, you were encouraged to write your own funeral sermon. Perhaps using that as a guide, rewrite what mark you want to leave in this world. Then explain why that mark is important to you, and who will be impacted by your mark.

" THE MARK I WANT TO LEAVE IN THIS WORLD IS: _____

_____

THE REASON THIS IS MY MARK IS BECAUSE: _____

_____

THOSE WHO WILL BE IMPACTED THE MOST BY MY MARK ARE: _____

_____

THE NEXT STEP THAT I CAN TAKE TODAY TO ACCOMPLISH THIS MARK IS:

_____

THIS MARK WILL BRING GLORY TO GOD BY: _____

_____ "

Your challenge is to take the step that you just named today.

35/40

DAY 36

PITMASTER JESUS

A typical person will spend over 35,000 hours in their life eating food. That equals nine years of eating non-stop for 12 hours a day.[69]

What's more, the average American will consume 1,996.3 pounds of food every year. To put that into perspective, that's 3.7 pounds less than a ton…so when someone says, "Man I feel like I ate a ton," they literally have in the last year.[70]

Ten percent of our disposable income is spent on fast food, 20 percent of American meals are eaten in a car, and over 10 billion donuts are consumed in the United States every year![71]

That's a lot of food.

This past Christmas, my wife blessed me with an amazing gift: a Traeger wood pellet smoker! I've had a lot of fun learning how to smoke different types of meat. Over the course of the past few months, I've learned the art of "low and slow," doing my best to perfect ribs, pulled pork, and brisket. I made my first smoked turkey on Easter, and I don't think we'll ever go back to the traditional route again. I've made bacon-wrapped sausage pig shots, elk-smoked jalapeno poppers, and I found I can make Cheez-Its even more delectable by throwing them on the smoker for a couple of hours!

I have about ten pastor friends who also have wood pellet smokers, and we started a text-thread group called "Pitmasters of Divinity." As part of the group, there's an unwritten rule that you must not only smoke the meat, but you must send pictures as well. Most of these pastors, including yours truly, are pretty competitive and will try to outdo one another. But every now and then, you know you've done well when someone texts back and labels you a "Pitmaster."

The title of Pitmaster is reserved for the head barbecuing chef. Often, this person is the sweaty, greasy, will-do-whatever-it-takes barbecue craftsman who presides over the red-hot coals to create smoky, char-encrusted proteins of perfection.[72]

There has long been debate on the most important meal of the day. Many think it is breakfast, but I have a little different view. I think the most important meal of the day is whichever one tastes the best!

For Peter, the most important meal of his life was certainly the meal by the charcoal fire. For anyone who is wondering, this meal was at breakfast time...so maybe that solves it. This meal was cooked by none other than Pitmaster Jesus.

When Peter came running onto the shore, Pitmaster Jesus had already been smoking fish over an open flame, recreating Peter's pitiful moment around the first charcoal fire. For this meal, Jesus already had the fish and the bread. He had all the food that He needed. And yet, Jesus tells the disciples, **"Bring some of the fish you have just caught."** Look at what happens:

> **"So Simon Peter climbed back into the boat and dragged the net ashore. It was full of large fish, 153, but even with so many the net was not torn."**
> **John 21:11**

The average fish would have been between 1 and 2 pounds, so Peter likely dragged around 250 pounds of fish to Jesus! The net may not have ripped, but Peter sure must've been ripped to drag that much weight!

I've been fascinated with the number of fish—153. Why include this odd number in the story? The number is very specific, and it's the only time the number 153 is mentioned in the Bible. For months, I tried to find the hidden meaning in this and discover something that would change the world. Commentators and scholars have been trying for centuries, so I decided to really dig into this number. What could it mean?

I thought I had a breakthrough early on when I was thinking of Jesus's ministry. We always hear that His ministry was three years long, which is a total of 156 weeks. For the first five weeks, he was in the desert tempted by the devil, so if we don't count those, that brings it down to 151 weeks. This incident on the shore likely happened two weeks after Jesus rose from the dead; so add in those weeks, and you have 153. Maybe 153 is the number of weeks Peter had followed Jesus. Maybe Jesus was inviting Peter to bring all 153 weeks to the Lord, along with any baggage he'd picked up along the way. *Wow*, I thought, *I solved it!* Except I didn't. Through deeper research, I found out that Jesus's ministry was much closer to three-and-a-half-years, not three years. So that didn't work.

How about this? In the Bible, the number 5 represents grace. How about "1 man's sacrifice brought grace, 5, for all 3 of your denials Peter." Maybe? Is that the significance?

Then I discovered that the church father Jerome said the number represented 153 different types of fish in the world in that day, and miraculously the net was filled with all 153 types. This would have signified to Peter how he would be a fisher of men to the whole world.[73] So cool!

What do you think? Is this sounding a bit fishy to you? I agree.

This is what most scholars really believe the number 153 means: nothing. It simply means that someone counted the fish to sell them to the markets. That makes sense, right?

After pondering this for months, I do believe 153 is a significant insignificant number.

The number 153 represents a lot of fish. I believe God is showing us that we all have a "153." But God doesn't need our "153" in order to cook a meal. It's less about the number and more about the invitation. God doesn't need the disciples' fish for the breakfast. He's already made it for them. But He still invites them to bring what they have caught to the meal.

At the end of the day, this is true for you and me. God doesn't need our gifts or talents. But He invites us to bring them to Him regardless. He will accomplish what He wants to accomplish, but amazingly, He gives us the opportunity to be a part of His story. He really, really will do anything to show us this truth.

He'll even descend down into a pit to come and get you out of the mess you've made. Psalm 40:1-2 says:

> **"I waited patiently for the Lord;**
> **he turned to me and heard my cry.**
> **He lifted me out of the slimy pit,**
> **out of the mud and mire;**
> **he set my feet on a rock**
> **and gave me a firm place to stand."**

Jesus does His best work in the pit. He will rescue you out of the pit and get you while you are at your least. He will be there by the seashore cooking a feast over an open flame, inviting you to cook with Him.

He invites the least to the feast.

The most important meal of Peter's life was one in which Jesus provided food and also provided a new opportunity to cook together. So don't waste the "153" that God entrusts to you. Bring all of it to Pitmaster Jesus and partner with Him and see the amazing miracles that God will do through you!

CHALLENGE

WHAT'S YOUR 153?

Peter would go on to write these words in 1 Peter 4:10: **"Each of you should use whatever gift you have received to serve others, as faithful stewards of God's grace in its various forms."** Every one of us has a spiritual gift, but not one of us has every single spiritual gift.* We have all been uniquely made, designed, and wired. On top of that, all of the people in our lives have influenced us, shaped us, and brought us to where we are today in our stories. Knowing this, answer the following questions:

What is unique about your story?

_____

What are the top spiritual gifts that God has given to you?

_____

Just as Peter brought 153 fish to the fire that Jesus had already started, what do you feel that God wants you to bring to the table? Write this on the fish below.

*For more on spiritual gifts, read 1 Corinthians 12. Also, visit this website **www.redletterchallenge. com/spiritual-gifts** for a link to find a spiritual gift test.

36/40

DAY 37

SCARS TO STARS

As we enter back into Peter's story in this final week, we see that the table has been beautifully set for him. Jesus has invited him back into relationship, as well as into a life of meaning and purpose in this world. Will Peter take the hand of Jesus and walk step-by-step with Him into the future? We don't have to guess because the next chapters of Peter's story are written down for all of the world to see.

Directly after #Chapter89 is a book called "The Acts of the Apostles," more commonly referred to as "Acts." This book records the history of the early church and the spread of Christianity after the death, resurrection, and ascension of Jesus. While there are many characters in Acts, the central figure of the first twelve chapters is, in fact, Peter.

I love the way the Bible is laid out. We just have to flip one page from #Chapter89 to see Peter stepping up into His fully restored life in Acts.

Likely there were several more moments, conversations, and meetings that Peter and Jesus had between the charcoal fire on the beach in John 21 and Jesus's ascension in Acts 1. But although we don't know what happened in those moments, we do know that Peter became the leader that Jesus always knew he would be. While we can already see Peter's leadership skills on display by the end of the first chapter of Acts, it's what happens in Acts 2 that shows how free Peter truly is.

The twelve disciples were gathered together. This time, they weren't locked in a room quarantining out of fear, but rather, gathering publicly for all to see. In fact, it was Pentecost Sunday, a Jewish holiday that would bring many Jewish people from all the nations together in the city of Jerusalem. Just as Jesus promised, God poured out His Holy Spirit on the disciples in a new, fresh way that day. Acts 2:4 says, **"All of them were filled with the Holy Spirit and began to speak in other tongues as the Spirit enabled them."**

From there, much chaos ensued because Jews from all over the world began hearing the disciples speaking in their own native language. How is this possible? Many were amazed and perplexed, but, **"Some, however, made fun of them and said, 'They have had too much wine.'" Acts 2:13**

In the midst of the chaos, we get this powerful verse: **"Then Peter stood up with the Eleven, raised his voice and addressed the crowd." Acts 2:14a**

From there, Peter boldly, powerfully, and beautifully delivers a sermon. In this message, he weaves together how the Old Testament history and prophecy all point to Jesus. He discusses in detail the life, death, and resurrection of Jesus. He passionately proclaims in his conclusion, **"Therefore let all Israel be assured of this: God has made this Jesus, whom you crucified, both Lord and Messiah." Acts 2:36**

In the wake of Peter's sermon, people were repentant and responsive. Acts 2:41 says that more than 3,000 people received his message that day, became baptized, and began following Jesus. The church, which was only 120 people strong in Acts chapter 1, is now more than 3,120 strong!

What an amazing day! What an amazing sermon! What an amazing outcome!

What I find most powerful, though, is how Jesus used the ultimate weakness of Peter to become his ultimate strength. It was Peter's mouth that got him into trouble. It was also through Peter's mouth that more than 3,000 people were brought to freedom that day, and the first church began to multiply!

This wasn't a long process over a decade of slowly improving and progressing until Peter reached this moment. No, he delivered this message only fifty days after the resurrection of Jesus, only fifty-two days after Peter couldn't say the name "Jesus" in front of one single solitary servant girl. This coward in front of one servant girl was now courageous before a crowd of thousands! What's more, Peter did a lot of his speaking at "Solomon's Colonnade," which was found on the temple grounds— the heart of the Jewish world. How is this possible? Peter had become free.

This story shows us that God can bring beauty out of even the ugliest parts of our stories.

Oftentimes, God will offer you the opportunity to use the sins of your past that held you back to be an instrument to help bring freedom to others. We ought to never celebrate or glorify our sin, obviously, but in the totally free life that God provides, you can take the sins of your past and turn them against the enemy. God doesn't waste anything.

Real freedom comes when you take the things that were against you in the past to help free others in the future. I talked with a friend who was once an addict but now leading a powerful recovery ministry, and it turns out that his past is a crucial piece of his program. So many recovery programs talk about what not to do, what

YOUR **PAIN** DOES HAVE A **PURPOSE.**

YOUR **MESS** WILL PRODUCE A **MESSAGE.**

YOUR **TESTS** WILL STRENGTHEN YOUR **TESTIMONY.**

YOUR **SETBACK** WILL OFFER AN INCREDIBLE **COMEBACK.**

YOUR **STITCHES** WILL WRITE A BEAUTIFUL **STORY.**

YOUR **WEAKNESS** CAN BECOME YOUR **GREATEST WITNESS.**

#FORGIVINGCHALLENGE

to stop, and how to quit cold-turkey. Few, however, place emphasis on what to do now, the next steps to take, and how to use your past to actually help others. This is where the real freedom comes.

Sometimes, the most helpful way to get over your past is to think of others and simply start serving them. If you don't replace what was old with something new, then it's a lot easier to fall back into the same patterns.

Jesus was hoisted on an instrument of death called a cross. But the cross, which was meant to destroy Jesus, became the instrument that produced our victory. He turned what the enemy brought against Him to not only destroy the enemy but to bring freedom to all of us!

The combination of forgiveness at the charcoal fire in John 21 with power from the Holy Spirit fire in Acts 2 transformed Peter into an unstoppable force.

If God did this for Peter, He'll do it for you too!

Jesus gives you forgiveness, and He gives you His Holy Spirit. Ultimate freedom can only come through Jesus, but He chooses to work through ordinary, forgiven followers to do extraordinary things. Peter was arrested multiple times for preaching the word of Jesus, but each time he popped right back to the temple and started preaching again. He was a changed man! In one instance, all of the disciples were flogged with the notorious "40 minus 1" cracks of the whip, leaving horrifying scars.

Scars may leave a mark, but through Jesus, those scars will turn into the brightest shining stars to help bring freedom to others.

CHALLENGE

WEAPON-FLIPPING TIME!

Get out your Bibles and read the story of God sending the Holy Spirit, the church beginning, and Peter preaching in Acts 2.

1 What sticks out to you most in this chapter?

_____

2 As Peter used the same weapon that got him into bondage to bring freedom to others, what weapons of the enemy can you flip to bring freedom to others?

_____

3 What is it about you or your personality, which the enemy has used against you, that you can flip to bring glory to God?

_____

4 What scars in your life can God turn into bright shining stars?

_____

5 What is one step you can take today to use what was "against you" in the past to bring freedom to others today? Your challenge is to take this step today.

_____

_____

37/40

DAY 38

WAX ON, WAX OFF

There is an interesting dynamic going on between two of Jesus's right-hand men, Peter and John. In the final chapters of John's Gospel, there are several instances where we can see some of the rivalry, whether friendly or unfriendly, play out between these two.

- While all four Gospels document the story of a disciple cutting off the ear of a soldier in the Garden of Gethsemane, only John's Gospel specifically names Peter.

- In John 20, there's also this weird detail about John outrunning Peter in a footrace to the tomb.

- In both John 20 and 21, John describes Himself as "the disciple whom Jesus loved."

- In John 21, we see that it was John who first knew it was Jesus standing on the shore.

In all of these cases, it's almost as if John is subtly putting Peter is a bad light and himself in a positive light. But there's one final exchange in the 89th chapter (John 21) where we see this dynamic come into play. These verses come directly after Jesus fully restored Peter, predicted his death, and gave His final command, **"Follow Me."**

"Peter turned and saw that the disciple whom Jesus loved was following them. (This was the one who had leaned back against Jesus at the supper and had said, 'Lord, who is going to betray you?') When Peter saw him, he asked, 'Lord, what about him?'

"Jesus answered, 'If I want him to remain alive until I return, what is that to you? You must follow me.' **John 21:20-22**

I remember growing up watching a classic movie *What About Bob?* This is Peter saying, "What about John?" Right after the extremely touching moment of forgiveness and full restoration, what is the first thing Peter does? He fails the very first test. Rather than being grateful and stepping into the life that Jesus had won for him, instead he focuses on John. His first response was not to say "Yes" to Jesus, but instead he turned around and looked at John, wondering aloud what following Jesus meant for John's life.

Peter shifted his eyes from Jesus to John. But when we take our eyes off of Jesus and place them anywhere else, we are prone to fall down, miss the mark, or veer down paths we were never meant to walk. As you go about your life and walk in the freedom that God has given to you through Jesus, it will be tempting to wonder and worry about others. What are they doing? What is Jesus requiring of them?

Charles Spurgeon would say of these verses, "I have come to the conclusion that, instead of trying to set all my Master's servants right at once, my first and most important work is to follow my Lord; and I think, my brother, that it will be wise for you to come to the same conclusion."[74]

Even after yet another blunder, Jesus's final spoken words of #Chapter89 are, **"You must follow me."** Jesus reminds Peter that what He asks or requires of others is none of his business. He makes the command personal and emphatic this time with the use of the second person pronoun. Quit worrying and wondering about others; "you" are to step into this call that I've given to you over and over and over again.

As you step into God's calling, it's important you understand that you will take steps forward, but you will also take steps backward. Make no mistake about it: God's grace will allow us to advance further than we've ever gone before, but it will never be a straight line.

I have met many addicts who have a goal to live sober. Some of them set out on this path and do really well. They might have 87 days of being sober. But on Day 88, they miss the mark and have a drink, or several drinks. They fail. It's what happens on Day 89 that makes all the difference. Jon Acuff, in his book *Finish*, calls this the day after perfection. Statistically, this is the day when people either give up altogether on their goals or get back on the right path. He says, "The harder you try to be perfect, the less likely you'll accomplish your goals."[75]

You still have an adversary fighting against you in this world. And the devil knows from your past where you are most vulnerable. He will attack you there again. Know that the battle will continue. But, in the words of Mike Foster, "Let our accuser sling the lies, indict our name, and denounce our faithless hearts. Blacklist us, shame us, and let our good deeds be shown for what they are: filthy rags stained with blood. For no matter what the accuser impeaches on us, we will be vindicated by Jesus's audacious and unrelenting grace. He crushes judgment with His great love."[76]

On Day 24, I introduced you to sensei Mr. Miyagi from *The Karate Kid*. His most famous line, which he used to teach his prized student, Danny LaRusso, was "wax on, wax off." I have learned that the process of scrubbing cars is a lot like the process of sanctification. It's all about the wax.

GOD'S GRACE WILL ALLOW US TO ADVANCE FURTHER THAN WE'VE EVER GONE BEFORE, BUT IT WILL NEVER BE A STRAIGHT LINE.

#FORGIVINGCHALLENGE

Did you know that the English word "sincere" comes from two Latin words, *sine* and *cera*? The translation for those two words is "without wax." *Sine cera* was an expression used by pottery makers. At the time of Jesus and Peter, dishonest dealers would accept cracked figurines and fill the cracks with wax to hide the flaws before offering them for sale. But honest merchants would display their uncracked pottery with signs that read, *sine cera*, or "without wax." In other words, their pottery was not cracked or broken in any way.[77]

Truthfully, if we are pieces of pottery, then we are not "sincere." Our sin has exposed our cracks, and many of us have broken under the weight of that sin. Sanctification is a continual process of "wax on, wax off." Our sin keeps putting wax on us, trying to hide our cracks. But because Jesus is walking with us, He keeps taking that wax off, bringing our sins to light.

Jesus takes us as broken and as cracked as we are, and the Great Restorer fills in those gaps with His grace so we can be made whole again.

All of us broken and cracked people have now been made perfect. If you are in Christ, when God the Father looks at you, He doesn't see you for your faults, your mistakes, and your cracks. Instead, He sees you as perfect. In Christ, you are truly "without wax." So don't worry and wonder about what following Jesus looks like for someone else. Receive the beautiful invitation to be your own beautiful and perfectly sincere masterpiece of God.

Freedom in this world will never be found in walking perfectly; it'll always be found in God, who has more than enough grace for you. Just as Jesus was right there to put His wax back on Peter to make him whole again, He's there to do the same for you. Keep walking without wax and leave the repairs to Jesus, the Master Restorer.

CHALLENGE

RECOGNIZING GOD'S VOICE

Read Romans 7:15-25. In this passage, you can see the internal struggle that a post-converted Paul is still undergoing because, after all, walking with Jesus is not a straight line. Likewise, your freedom is not found in perfectly walking with Jesus; it's found in your ability to continually rely on the grace of Jesus.

Let's see if you can recognize God's voice from the enemy's voice. Circle the truths that God is whispering to you and cross out the lies the enemy is shouting at you.

YOU CAN'T DO IT.

YOU ARE LOVED AND LOVABLE.

YOU WILL NEVER AMOUNT TO ANYTHING.

YOU GAVE EVERYTHING AND STILL FELL SHORT.

YOU ARE TAKING STEPS IN THE RIGHT DIRECTION.

I FORGIVE YOU.

YOU LET GOD DOWN FOR GOOD.

YOU ARE VALUABLE.

LET'S KEEP WALKING TOGETHER.

I'VE GOT BIG PLANS FOR YOU.

YOU ARE A FAILURE.

38/40

DAY 39

PETER'S NEW CHAPTERS

On Day 37, I mentioned how God used the thing that could have destroyed Peter to be the instrument that delivered many others to freedom—his voice. While this moment in Acts 2 was a beautiful display of what true freedom looks like, it was the rest of Peter's life that gives me full hope and confidence. His life proves that you can have more than one single solitary good moment. You can continually walk in the freedom God has for you.

When it comes to freedom and forgiveness, one important word we haven't elaborated on much is "repentance." Back on Day 2, we mentioned that the word "repent" means to turn away, or to change. Jesus's first recorded words in His ministry are from Matthew 4:17: **"Repent, for the kingdom of heaven has come near."**

Jesus declares that to be His follower means that you turn away from the ways of the world and turn toward Him.

I believe that when we confess our sins, most of us desire to change, to turn, and to be different. But where we see repentance actually come to fruition is in how we live out our lives. Peter truly changed. Peter truly repented.

While history may equate Peter forever with his big blunders, I hope that after today you would see him as the "big boulder" that Jesus knew he would become.

After preaching a life-changing message in Acts 2, Peter would go on to lead the first church. Just as Jesus performed signs and wonders, the first half of the book of Acts is filled with signs and wonders that God performed through Peter. As God worked in and with him, the early church multiplied from 120 disciples (Acts 1:15) to tens of thousands (Acts 21:20) in a span of just two decades.

Not only did the church multiply numerically, but the healthy marks of the early church (fellowship, generosity, attention to Bible and prayer, and meeting the needs of the community) still set the standard that many modern-day churches strive toward.

On top of this, in Acts chapters 10 to 12, Peter leads the charge to spread the Gospel to the Gentile people (something previously unheard of) and helped to send Paul on the first Christian missionary journey (Acts 13:1-3) to spread the Gospel to the world.

What a leader and what a pastor Peter would become! Peter had a lifetime of achievements for Jesus. This man would become a hero of our faith. Ultimately, one could argue that the church would not exist as it does today if Peter had not stepped into the life of freedom that Jesus invited him into.

As Peter walked with Jesus, he was met with much persecution. He was in and out of prison, not because he did anything wrong, but because he followed Jesus faithfully. Peter shows us that we can be free, even if we are imprisoned by the world. Freedom in this world looks much different than the total freedom that God gives to us. This man, who denied Jesus by the charcoal fire, proved time and time again that he should not be known as a denier, but instead as a devoted disciple, even if it cost him everything.

With the church multiplying and the Gospel spreading across the world, the church represented a direct threat to the kingdom of the mighty Roman emperor, Nero. History remembers Nero for many things, but chief among these was his hatred and persecution of Christians. Knowing Nero's character, it would make sense, then, that he would target the leader of the church.

History tells us that Peter was killed for his faith in Jesus. Tradition says that Peter was led to be crucified, and he died in the same manner as his Lord, Savior, and Friend. As they were nailing him to a cross, however, Peter deemed himself unworthy to die in the exact same manner as Jesus, so he requested to be hung upside-down on the cross. As he hung upside down on that cross, Peter, the rock, fulfilled in that moment the very thing he proclaimed at the Last Supper: "I will die for you." Peter was faithful to the end.

How do you see Peter today?

Many churches today, even hospitals, schools, and universities, bear the name of St. Peter. However, I don't think Peter cared about how he went down in history. All that mattered to him was not how history would remember him, but how history would remember Jesus. What was most important to Peter was not how you see him but how you see Jesus.

How do I know this?

There are four Gospel accounts of the life of Jesus packed with 89 amazing chapters: Matthew, Mark, Luke, and John. Scholars believe that despite the order in which they currently reside in our Bibles, the Gospel of Mark was the first one written. This is important because much of the other Gospels (especially Matthew and Luke) borrow from Mark. If you've ever wondered why many of the same stories are described in multiple Gospels, it is likely because the other Gospel writers borrowed from Mark. Each of these Gospel accounts offer unique qualities and specifics, but they share many similarities.

Church tradition and early church fathers unanimously tell us that Mark was not an eyewitness to the life of Jesus. How then did he record such detailed accounts of the life and Good News of Jesus? An eyewitness told the stories to Mark, who wrote them down. What is fascinating, though, is who the early church fathers, such as Papias, Eusebius, Irenaeus, Clement, Tertullian, and Origen, claim was the one who told Mark the story of Jesus. They all say that the Gospel of Mark was based on the eyewitness account of none other than Peter himself.

Here is what Irenaeus says: "Mark, the disciple and interpreter of Peter, did also hand down to us in writing what had been preached by Peter."[78]

This would mean that much of the four Gospels of Jesus originated from the mouth of Peter. Amazingly, what you see in Peter's own retelling of the story of Jesus is a man who has become so content and free with his past that he doesn't mind bringing up stories of his own foolishness and weakness so that you would see God's grace and power more clearly.

Even if you go against the church fathers and history, remember that Peter held the most influential position in the early church. If he didn't want his weaknesses to be exposed to the world, he could have stopped these stories from being included in the grand story of Jesus. The Bible is God's Word, but it was given and passed down to us by ordinary human beings.

That leads me to this incredible conclusion: The only way we know about the blunders of Peter is because Peter told others about them. What kind of man would let the world see his foolishness? What kind of man would so freely talk about his big blunders? Only the big boulder. Only someone who has become completely and totally content with the freedom that comes through Jesus Christ. Only someone who has turned away from his wicked ways and is walking with Jesus. Can you be any freer than this?

Peter told these stories of him at his worst so you could see the best in Jesus.

FUTURE CHAPTERS

Seeing the life and legacy of Peter play out may inspire you to think about your own life and legacy. You've already been doing this at several places on the journey. On Day 7, you wrote your own funeral sermon. Then, on Day 29, you named some chapters of your life that have already taken place. Finally, on Day 35, you wrote about what "mark" you want to leave in this world. With that end in mind, write the heading or title of the remaining chapters in your life. Write three chapter titles.

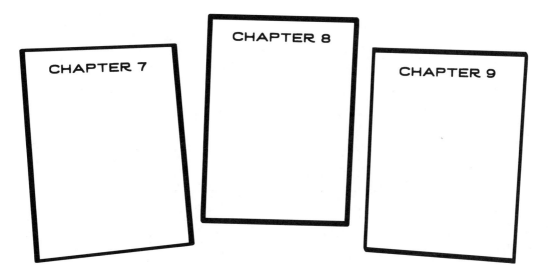

CHAPTER 8

CHAPTER 7

CHAPTER 9

Why did you choose those titles? What needs to happen for those titles to come to fruition?

39/40

DAY 40

BE FREE

Wow! We are all the way to Day 40, and I have one last confession to make.

Writing this book has been one of the most humbling experiences of my entire lifetime.

It is humbling because I'm not even sure my initial premise for writing the book was truly ever valid. For a lifelong believer in Jesus and someone who has been in ministry for more than a decade, I'm a bit embarrassed that I didn't know better from the start. Let me explain.

I started writing *Forgiving Challenge* in an effort to ultimately see if I could help people come to forgive themselves. I thought that if I could teach you how to forgive yourself, then you can finally be free. Much of our culture and our media share that sort of language. To truly be free, you have to let go of your past. You need to learn how to be comfortable in your own skin.

Many famous quotes push us toward this thinking:

Maya Angelou, the great civil rights activist and poet, said, "Forgiveness is the greatest gift you can give yourself."[79]

The Dalai Lama said, "We can never obtain peace in the outer world until we make peace with ourselves."[80]

What I have found, however, is that my original premise for how to ultimately be free was wrong. Here's why: Self-forgiveness is a noble pursuit, but if you are looking to find freedom through self-forgiveness, it will always disappoint you.

We should always be generous in our efforts to speak God's grace over our own lives. Although we can continually grow in self-forgiveness, until Jesus comes back, we will never fully, once-for-all-time, master self-forgiveness. You can have good days, months, or seasons, but you might also have a day, month, or season that's not so good.

And then what? Are you not free?

Writing this book has not only been one of the most humbling experiences for me, but it's been one of the most freeing experiences as well. Through all of my studying, research, and writing, I am left at the end squarely where I needed to have been all along. Back to Jesus.

Here's what I have rediscovered in writing this 40-day challenge: Your freedom is never based on what you do. It is always based on what Jesus has already done!

Jesus has forgiven you. Your freedom does not come from self-forgiveness—an act that you do. Freedom comes from God's forgiveness. Self-forgiveness as the end goal to becoming free is a dead-end.

You will not always get it right when it comes to forgiving yourself. So give yourself some grace. Cut yourself some slack. Don't hear me wrong: You can improve in this area. You can be more loving and gracious to yourself. Humility can start to overtake pride. Confidence and certainty can take over for unbelief and doubt. All of these things are possible. But when you have a bad moment and cannot forgive yourself, trust that even that moment is still covered by God's grace. Then keep moving.

It's God's grace, not your perfection, that allows you to be free.

Far more important than your own forgiveness of yourself is God's forgiveness for you. Forgiveness is not the greatest gift you can give yourself; it is the greatest gift that God can give you.

Whenever you place the emphasis on yourself for your own freedom, you will never be free.

Matt Chandler writes, "Over the course of your lifetime who has lied to you, and fought you, and failed you, and disgusted you more than you have? Right? And that's the person you're counting on to come to your rescue? That's the one who's going to figure it all out and turn things around for you? Serious? An improved version of you? As long as you keep looking to yourself as your next best solution, you will never stop vacuuming up the mess you leave behind."[81]

Self-forgiveness is a great blessing from God, but an even greater blessing is His forgiveness. The amazing thing about this blessing is that it's already been given to you. It was given to you, not at a time when you deserved or earned it, but simply because God deeply and greatly loves you.

Romans 5:8 says, **"But God demonstrated His love for us in this: While we were still sinners, Christ died for us."**

Give up on the idea that you can only be free when you are able to fully, once-for-all-time forgive yourself. Stop beating yourself up and simply receive this beautiful gift of grace, which God wants you to have today. Trust that when you can't fully forgive yourself, someone else already has. His name is Jesus, and ultimately, He is the only who can give you the fully free, abundant life.

Even in the days, moments, or seasons when you may not feel free, that doesn't mean you are not free. Remember, feelings are real, but it does not mean that they are true. Instead, trust in the promise and truth of God found in John 8:36: **"So if the Son sets you free, you will be free indeed!"**

In the meantime, remember what we said early on. Two steps forward and one step backward is still one beautiful step forward. And God is so proud of you. He loves you so much.

In the future, when you take a step that you shouldn't have taken, come back to the charcoal fire again, rather than spiral downward with self-reproach. Run for the shore, where Jesus is waiting, with fresh fish cooking on the fire. Sit down before the Master and let Him feed you. Let Him forgive you. Experience God's kindness and grace once again. Trust that no matter how many times you need to come back, Jesus will always be there, waiting for you on the shore.

Thanks for going on this journey with me. I am proud of you, but far more importantly, God is proud of you. You did a good thing.

But before I leave you on your journey, let's do one last thing together. Finish this Freedom Certificate designed just for you.

YOU ARE FREE!

Fill-in the certificate with your name. Take a photo and share it on social media using the hashtag **#ForgivingChallenge**. If you'd like a free, downloadable printout version of this certificate, please visit **www.forgivingchallenge.com/resources**.

40/40

TETELESTAI

CERTIFICATE OF FREEDOM

I, _____, AM FREE!

Congratulations, you have completed the 40-day journey leading to freedom. In this journey, you have walked through all 5 Phases Leading to Freedom: Sin, Confession, Absolution, Restoration, and Sanctification (SCARS). I announce to you that you are forgiven by God the Father. This forgiveness was bought and paid in full by the blood of Jesus. It has been given to you through the power of the Holy Spirit. You are free.

Zach Zehnder

Zach Zehnder

GOD

God

P.S. I love you. I'm proud of you.
Now come, follow me.

THE FINAL CHALLENGE

Peter would go on to write some amazing words that are recorded for us in the Bible. He says in 1 Peter 2:9-10:

> **"But you are a chosen people, a royal priesthood, a holy nation, God's special possession, that you may declare the praises of him who called you out of darkness into his wonderful light. Once you were not a people, but now you are the people of God; once you had not received mercy, but now you have received mercy."**

There you have it. You are chosen, royal, holy, and special. On top of that, you—the one who has received mercy—are a messenger of God in this world. He has called you to go and share this light with others. The time for you to step into this calling has never been more pressing than right now.

As I said at the beginning of this book, one of the most common words used to describe Christians is that we are judgmental. We are not known for being a forgiving people. It's time for that to change! In the Lord's Prayer, Jesus said that we should pray these words: **"Forgive us our debts, as we also have forgiven our debtors."** Matthew 6:12

We forgive others as God has forgiven us. This book was written because many of us have a harder time dealing with our own forgiveness than we do forgiving others. Therefore, I wanted to help people know that they are truly forgiven by God. I believe that once you know you have received God's forgiveness, you can't help but become a forgiving person yourself. His grace and kindness in our lives is contagious.

Forgiven people become forgiving people.

That's my final challenge to you. Take the very forgiveness that Jesus has given to you and give it away to others. Go and forgive others. Although forgiveness is good for everybody, forgiven people ought always to take the first step. Let's not wait and withhold forgiveness until the time is just right, but rather, let's go and give it away today.

Levi Lusko writes, "You have to win the war inside before you can win the war outside."[82] Jesus has already won the war for us. Now let's go and multiply that victory.

FORGIVEN PEOPLE BECOME FORGIVING PEOPLE.

#FORGIVINGCHALLENGE

CHALLENGE

FORGIVING OTHERS CHALLENGE

Who do you need to forgive? Write down the names of people God is putting on your heart to forgive. Who on this list owes a debt to you that you can agree to forgive right now? To whom are you holding anger or resentment that you can let go of today?

Pray by name for each of the people you need to forgive. Ask God for the power to forgive them, just as He has forgiven you. Ask God what specific step(s) you need to take in regard to each person on this list for you to continue to walk in freedom.

Much more could be said on how to forgive others.

Go to **www.ForgivingOthersChallenge.com** to continue the forgiveness journey. There you will find an ebook called *Forgiving Others Challenge: A 10-Day Challenge to Help You Forgive Others.* If you enter the code **"IAMFREE"** at checkout, you will receive this ebook for **FREE.** Consider this my gift to you for going on this journey together.

God bless you!

ABOUT THE AUTHOR

Zach Zehnder is a husband, father, speaker, author, and pastor. He is married to Allison Zehnder, and they have two boys, Nathan and Brady.

His life mission is to challenge people of all ages to become greater followers of Jesus.

One of Zach's more notable accomplishments was in November 2014. He preached a sermon that lasted for 53 hours and 18 minutes. In doing this, he broke the Guinness World Record for the Longest Speech Marathon. The event raised enough money to purchase a home, which was given to Hand in Hand of Lake County, Florida, a ministry that helps addicts recover.

In 2017, Zach finished what would become the bestselling book, *Red Letter Challenge*. In 2019, his wife, Allison, led the charge in writing *Red Letter Challenge Kids*. Zach and Allison continue to write books and speak about the importance of following Jesus.

Zach currently serves as President of Red Letter Living, LLC, and as a Teaching Pastor at King of Kings Church in Omaha, Nebraska.

Read more about Zach or request him to speak at your conference, church, or event at **www.redletterchallenge.com/zach**.

BIBLIOGRAPHY

[1] Mathis, David. "His Scars Will Never Fade." Web. 8 May 2021, Web. Accessed 6 April 2021.

[2] Lewis, C.S. "C.S. Lewis Quotes." Web. Accessed 6 April 2021.

[3] Diaz, Pablo. "The Healing Power of Forgiveness." *Guideposts*, 24 Sept. 2015. Web. Accessed 6 April 2021.

[4] Bacon, Francis. "Forbes Quotes: Thoughts on the Business of Life." Web. Accessed 6 April 2021.

[5] Elevation Worship. "Raised to Life. " CCLI #7011534. Web. Accessed 6 April, 2021.

[6] "In U.S., Decline of Christianity Continues at Rapid Pace." 17 Oct. 2019. Web. Accessed 6 Nov. 2020.

[7] Lifeway Research. "This Week's Shocking Statistic." Web. Accessed 6 April 2021.

[8] Stanley, Andy. *Enemies of the Heart*. Multnomah, 2011.

[9] Chandler, Matt. *Recovering Redemption*. B&H Publishing Group, 2014. Page 17.

[10] Chandler, Matt. "Recovering Redemption (Part 4)——The Result: Justification, Adoption and Sanctification." 23 Jan. 2014. YouTube video. Web. Accessed 6 April 2021.

[11] "What does the Greek word "Tetelestai" mean?" Bible.org. Web. Accessed 6 April 2021.

[12] Keller, Timothy J. "Romans 1-7 for You Quotes." Goodreads. Web. Accessed 6 April 2021.

[13] Monico, Nicolle & Thomas, Scot M.D. "The 12 Steps of Alcoholics Anonymous (AA)." 16 Oct. 2020. Web. Accessed 6 April 2020.

[14] Foster, Mike. *Freeway: A Not-So-Perfect Guide to Freedom*. People of the Second Chance, 2013. Page 26.

[15] Card, Michael. *A Fragile Stone: The Emotional Life of Simon Peter*. IVP Books, 2006. Page 15.

[16] Hamilton, Adam. *Simon Peter: Flawed but Faithful Disciple*. Abingdon Press, 2018. Page 14.

[17] "List of Long Place Names." Wikipedia. Web. Accessed 6 April 2021.

[18] Stiles, Wayne. "God Will Give You A New Name." Web. Accessed 4 Nov. 2020.

[19] Hamilton, Adam. *Simon Peter: Flawed but Faithful Disciple*. Abingdon, 2018. Page 27.

[20] Ibid, 21.

[21] Ibid, 9.

[22] "How to Write a Eulogy Speech." BurialPlanning.com. Web. Accessed 6 April 2021.

[23] Kolb, Robert, Wengert, Timothy J., editors. *The Book of Concord: The Confessions of the Evangelical Lutheran Church*. Fortress Press, 2005, Page 583.

[24] Foster, Mike. *Freeway: A Not-So-Perfect Guide to Freedom*. People of the Second Chance, 2013. Page 25.

[25] This test has been modified from an original test done by Flatirons Church in Denver, CO.

[26] Willard, Dallas. *The Great Omission: Reclaiming Jesus's Essential Teachings on Discipleship*. HarperOne, 2006. Introduction Flap.

[27] "What are the top 10 Phobias?" Anxietyhouse.com. Web. Accessed 6 April 2021.

[28] Whittaker, Carlos Enrique. *Kill the Spider.* Zondervan, 2017, Page 21.

[29] "What was the Holy of Holies?" Gotquestions.org. Web. Accessed 6 April 2021.

[30] "Did the high priest have a rope tied to him when he entered the Holy of Holies?" Gotquestions.org. Web. Accessed 6 April 2021.

[31] Tolkien, J.R.R. *The Tolkien Reader.* Ballantine Books, 1966. Pages 71-73.

[32] Brombley, Kate. "All is Discovered! Fly at Once!" 31 July 2014. Web. Accessed 6 April 2021.

[33] Zylstra, Sarah. "Lord, Have Mercy on 67% of Us." *Christianity Today.* 28 March 2018. Web. Accessed 6 April 2021.

[34] Ibid.

[35] Murray M'Cheyne, Robert. "Robert Murray M'Cheyne Quotes." Goodreads. Web. Accessed 6 April 2021.

[36] Chandler, Matt. *Recovering Redemption.* B&H Publishing Group, 2014. Page 52.

[37] Stuart, Ben. "On the Shore" *The Village Church.* 23 Feb. 2008. Web. Accessed 6 April 2021.

[38] Ibid.

[39] "What is the Significance of the Temple Veil Being Torn in Two?" Southwest Radio Church. Web. Accessed 6 April 2021.

[40] Foster, Mike. *Freeway: A Not-So-Perfect Guide to Freedom.* People of the Second Chance, 2013. Page 27.

[41] "Penitential Act." Wikipedia. Web. Accessed 6 April 2021.

[42] "Confession Definition." Google.com/search. Web. Accessed 17 May 2021.

[43] Im, Daniel. "Input vs. Output Goals for Discipleship. 15 Aug. 2017. Web. Accessed 6 Nov. 2020.

[44] Warren, Rick. "Face Your Feelings So You Can Be Free." PastorRick.com. 20 Sept. 2019. Web. Accessed 6 April 2021.

[45] Foster, Mike. *Freeway: A Not-So-Perfect Guide to Freedom.* People of the Second Chance, 2013. Page 83.

[46] Chandler, Matt. "The Mission of God." 14 Aug., 2011. Web. 6 April 2021.

[47] "Penitential Act." Wikipedia. Web. 6 April, 2021.

[48] "Jesus Paid It All: The Story Behind the Hymn." Independentbaptist.com. Web. Accessed 6 April 2021.

[49] Foster, Mike. *Freeway: A Not-So-Perfect Guide to Freedom.* People of the Second Chance, 2013. Page 137.

[50] Maglio, Tony. "'Cobra Kai' Season 3 Draws Big Viewership, but Nowhere Near 'Bridgerton' or 'Queen's Gambit.'" Thewrap.com. 12 Jan. 2021. Web. Accessed 6 April 2021.

[51] Guzik, David. "Mark 16: Jesus is Risen." Enduring Word. Web. Accessed 6 April 2021.

[52] Borresen, Kelsey. "This Is The Most Common of the 5 Love Languages." Huffpost.com. 23 July 2018. Web. Accessed 6 April 2021.

[53] Lusko, Levi. *I Declare War.* Thomas Nelson, 2018. Introduction, page XIX.

[54] Willard, Dallas. *The Divine Conspiracy: Rediscovering our Hidden Life in God.* HarperOne, 1997. Page 28.

55 Wright, N.T. "N.T. Wright Quotes." Goodreads. Web. Accessed 6 April 2021.

56 Ibid.

57 "Meet the Parents: Owen Wilson: Kevin Rawley." Imdb.com. Web. Accessed 6 April 2021.

58 "Tekton." Wikipedia. Web. Accessed 6 April 2021.

59 Galatty, Robby. "The Forgotten Jesus Part 2: Was Jesus a Carpenter or a Stonemason?" Web. Accessed 6 April 2021.

60 Ibid

61 Willard, Dallas. *The Divine Conspiracy: Rediscovering our Hidden Life in God.* HarperOne, 1997. Pages 94-95.

62 "The Sea of Galilee." Jesus.Christ.org. Web. Accessed 6 April, 2021.

63 Lusko, Levi. "I Woke Up Like This." Elevation Church. 29 Nov., 2020. Web. Accessed 6 April 2021.

64 Foster, Mike. *Freeway: A Not-So-Perfect Guide to Freedom.* People of the Second Chance, 2013. Page 29.

65 Copenhaver, Martin B. *Jesus is the Question.* Amazon. Web. Accessed 6 April 2021.

66 Watts, Jerry N. "Do You Love Me More Than These?" 3 Dec. 2014. Web. Accessed 6 April 2021.

67 Wright, N.T. *God and the Pandemic.* Zondervan, 2020. Web. 6 April 2021.

68 Foster, Mike. *Freeway: A Not-So-Perfect Guide to Freedom.* People of the Second Chance, 2013. Page 113.

69 Curtis, Gemma. "Your Life in Numbers." Dreams.uk.co. 29 Sept. 2017. Web. Accessed 6 April 2021.

70 "How Many Pounds of Food Does the Average Adult Eat in a Day?" Reference.com. 26 March 2020. Web. Accessed 6 April, 2021.

71 "11 Facts About American Eating Habits." Dosomething.org. Web. Accessed 6 April 2021.

72 Akkam, Alia. "BBQ Slang 101: How To Talk Like A Real-Life Pitmaster." Firstwefeast.com. 16 July 2015. Web. 6 April 2021.

73 "153 Fish: Problems with Church Father's Explanations." Defendingthebride.com. Web. Accessed 6 April 2021.

74 Guzik, David. "John 21: The Restoration of Peter." Enduringword.com. Web. Accessed 6 April 2021.

75 Acuff, Jonathan. *Finish: Give Yourself the Gift of Done.* Portfolio/Penguin, 2018. Pages 12-13.

76 Foster, Mike. *Freeway: A Not-So-Perfect Guide to Freedom.* People of the Second Chance, 2013. Page 163.

77 Bloom, Jon. "Live and Love Without Wax." DesiringGod.org. 6 Jan. 2012. Web. Accessed 6 April 2021.

78 Nelson, Ryan. "Who was John Mark? The Beginner's Guide." 17 April 2019. Web. Accessed 6 April 2021.

79 Savi, Riccardo. "Maya Angelou: 'Forgiveness Is the Greatest Gift You Can Give Yourself." EastIdahoNews.com. 24 Nov. 2013. Web. Accessed 6 April 2021.

80 Lama, Dalai. "Dalai Lama Quotes." Brainyqyote.com. Web. Accessed 6 April 2021.

81 Chandler, Matt. *Recovering Redemption.* B&H Publishing Group, 2014. Pages 27-28.

82 Lusko, Levi. *I Declare War.* Thomas Nelson, 2018. Page 155.

#CHAPTER89

JOHN 21:1-25

Afterward Jesus appeared again to his disciples, by the Sea of Galilee. It happened this way: Simon Peter, Thomas (also known as Didymus), Nathanael from Cana in Galilee, the sons of Zebedee, and two other disciples were together. "I'm going out to fish," Simon Peter told them, and they said, "We'll go with you." So they went out and got into the boat, but that night they caught nothing.

Early in the morning, Jesus stood on the shore, but the disciples did not realize that it was Jesus.

He called out to them, **"Friends, haven't you any fish?"**

"No," they answered.

He said, **"Throw your net on the right side of the boat and you will find some."** When they did, they were unable to haul the net in because of the large number of fish.

Then the disciple whom Jesus loved said to Peter, "It is the Lord!" As soon as Simon Peter heard him say, "It is the Lord," he wrapped his outer garment around him (for he had taken it off) and jumped into the water. The other disciples followed in the boat, towing the net full of fish, for they were not far from shore, about a hundred yards. When they landed, they saw a fire of burning coals there with fish on it, and some bread.

Jesus said to them, **"Bring some of the fish you have just caught."** So Simon Peter climbed back into the boat and dragged the net ashore. It was full of large fish, 153, but even with so many the net was not torn. Jesus said to them, **"Come and have breakfast."** None of the disciples dared ask him, "Who are you?" They knew it was the Lord. Jesus came, took the bread and gave it to them, and did the same with the fish. This was now the third time Jesus appeared to his disciples after he was raised from the dead.